THE DIAMOND RING BUYING GUIDE

How to Spot Value & Avoid Ripoffs

"**A valuable asset to the retail jewelry buyer** . . . **fact-filled, succinctly written** . . . Sellers concerned about 'shoddy competitors' might do themselves a favor by making this book available to those clients that are anxious to find that optimum blend of value, quality and service. This is a definite thumbs up!"

C. R. Beesley, President, American Gemological Laboratories, New York. *Jewelers' Circular-Keystone*

"**Will definitely help consumers** . . . Written in a popular style with lots of personalized examples, the book should be easy reading for young people who are thinking about their first diamond purchases."

Lapidary Journal

"**Filled with useful information, drawings, pictures, and short quizzes** . . . presents helpful suggestions on detecting diamond imitations, in addition to well-though-out discussions of diamond cutting, and how the various factors can influence value . . . a very readable way for the first-time diamond buyer to get acquainted with the often intimidating subject of purchasing a diamond."

Stephen C. Hofer, President, Colored Diamond Laboratory Services, *Jewelers' Circular Keystone*

"**Highly informative** . . . a useful book for the first-time diamond purchaser, the gemologist who needs a good review on diamonds, and the retailer seeking more information to give to customers."

GIA's *Gems & Gemology*

"**A wealth of information** . . . delves into the intricacies of shape, carat weight, color, clarity, setting style, and cut--happily avoiding all industry jargon and keeping explanations streamlined enough so even the first-time diamond buyer, can confidently choose a gem."

American Library Association's *Booklist*

THE DIAMOND RING BUYING GUIDE

How to Spot Value & Avoid Ripoffs

Fourth Edition

Text & Photographs

by

RENEE NEWMAN GG

International Jewelry Publications

Los Angeles

Copyright © 1989, 1991, 1992, & 1993
by International Jewelry Publications

First published 1989
Reprinted 1989
Second edition 1991
Third edition 1992
Fourth edition 1993

This publication is designed to provide information
in regard to the subject matter covered. It is sold with
the understanding that the publisher and author are
not engaged in rendering legal, financial, or other
professional services. If legal or other expert assistance
is required, the services of a competent professional
should be sought. International Jewelry Publications
and the author shall have neither liability nor
responsibility to any person or entity with respect to
any loss or damage caused or alleged to be caused
directly or indirectly by the information contained in
this book. All inquiries should be directed to:

International Jewelry Publications
P.O. Box 13384
Los Angeles, CA 90013-0384 USA

(Inquiries should be accompanied by a self-addressed,
stamped envelope).

Printed in the United States of America

Library of Congress Cataloging in Publication Data

Newman, Renee.
    The diamond ring buying guide : how to spot value
and avoid ripoffs / text & photographs by Renee
Newman. -- 4th ed.
        p.   cm.
    Includes bibliographical references and index.
    ISBN 0-929975-20-0 : $12.95
    1. Diamonds--Purchasing. 2. Rings--Purchasing.
I. Title.
TS753.N48   1993
736'.23'0297--dc20   93-9741
                                                    CIP

Cover design and photo by Wolf Pictures.
Diamond ring on front cover courtesy of the
Josam Diamond Trading Corporation.

Contents

Contents

Contents

Preface

Why did you recommend that jeweler? He ripped me off.

When I was a tour director, I dreaded getting such complaints. But even when I was convinced that a jeweler was reliable and offered good value, tour passengers would occasionally tell me I'd made a terrible recommendation.

In Hong Kong on the final night of a 24-day Orient tour I'd directed, an irate tour member showed me a jade ring she had just bought for $200. It looked almost like the ring that cost her $3000 at a store I had recommended. I knew very little then about evaluating jade, but I told her it was hard to believe that the rings were the same quality, and I reassured her that she could get her $3000 back if she were dissatisfied. Since the store I had recommended did not open before our flight back home, I suggested she have both rings appraised in the USA before returning the $3000 ring. She agreed to do this.

When I called the woman a month later to find out the results of the appraisal, she told me that the $3000 ring had been appraised at over $5000. The $200 ring had been appraised at less than $25. The storekeeper had not lied when he said the jade in the $200 ring was real. It was an inexpensive grayish-white jade that had been hollowed out and filled with a green jelly to make it look like a valuable green jade. The ring mounting, which was stamped 750 (18K), turned out to be gold plated.

I felt somewhat responsible for this woman wasting $200. I should have been more aware of the types of fraud that jewelry buyers can face, and I should have forewarned this woman of them.

This experience and similar ones led me to take gemology classes at the GIA (Gemological Institute of America) in Santa Monica, California. After two years of intermittent studies and classes there, I received my graduate gemologist diploma. I then decided to enter the wholesale diamond and jewelry trade.

Even though most of my contact is with jewelers, wholesalers, and jewelry manufacturers, I see and hear about the disappointments laypeople often have when buying jewelry. Besides being misled into believing they're buying better quality than what they actually receive, they sometimes buy jewelry that does not fit their needs.

This happened to me in Australia when I bought an opal ring. I didn't bother to tell the salesman that I wanted a ring for everyday wear, and he didn't ask me what it was for. I ended up buying a ring with a cluster of small opals because it was less expensive than rings with one large opal. Two months later, a small opal fell out and I noticed the ring was about to lose some others. I learned too late that the ring was impractical for everyday wear. Now it usually sits in a safe deposit box. Even though the ring was a good value in terms of price, it was a poor value in terms of practicality. I would have been better off paying more for a ring with one large, securely set opal.

The questions and comments of my passengers and my day-to-day experiences in the jewelry trade have made me realize that there is a need and a desire for books such as *The Diamond Ring Buying Guide*. A diamond ring is a major investment, and you can't afford to make the wrong choice. Now there is a guide that gives you the practical and technical information you need to make a wise selection. Use it along with the advice of your jeweler to help you find the diamond ring that will suit both your pocketbook and your needs.

Acknowledgements

I would like to express my appreciation to the following people for their contribution to *The Diamond Ring Buying Guide*:

Ernie and Regina Goldberger of the Josam Diamond Trading Corporation. This book could never have been written without the experience and knowledge I gained from working with them. Most of the diamonds pictured in this book are or were part of their collection.

Chuck Atmore, Shirley Bradshaw, Louise Harris, Susan B. Johnson, Caro Kostan, Peter Malnekoff, Marian Newton, Cassie Saget, and Dale Swanson. They have made valuable suggestions, corrections, and comments regarding the portions of the book they examined. They are not responsible for any possible errors, nor do they necessarily endorse the material contained in this book.

The teachers at the GIA. They have helped me obtain the technical background needed to write a book such as this. Their dedication and assistance extend well beyond class hours. The diamond diagrams in this book are courtesy of the GIA.

Garo Djiguerian, Garbis Mazmanian, and Carlos Pulido. They have provided me with first-hand information about diamond setting and jewelry craftsmanship.

Global Diamonds. The photographs of the Sculptaire diamonds were contributed by them.

Maria H. Hayes, Fred Kaplan, and Sally Wolf. They have devoted a great deal of attention to the production of this book.

Patricia S. Esparza. She has spent hours carefully editing *The Diamond Ring Buying Guide*. Because of her, both this book and my writing have greatly improved.

My sincere thanks to all of these contributors for their kindness and help.

1

Why Read a Whole Book Just to Buy a Diamond Ring?

SALE $1299
ONE-CARAT DIAMOND SOLITAIRE RINGS

Ken saw this ad as he was browsing through the newspaper. He thought it might be worth his while to check out the sale because in a month he planned on giving his girlfriend an engagement ring. The rings he had already looked at seemed ridiculously high-priced.

Ken was not cheap. In fact, he was happy to spend money on his future wife. He just saw no point in putting a few thousand dollars into a stone that served no functional purpose. To him, it would be much better to use the money for the down payment on a house or for something practical like a car, a computer, or a refrigerator. Furthermore, he felt that people who enjoyed wearing diamond jewelry were frivolous show-offs.

Ken's practicality was overshadowed by his desire to follow tradition, so he went to the jewelry store hoping to find a diamond ring for $1300. He was shown a variety of diamonds, which he looked at under a microscope. He picked one that seemed to have the fewest and smallest flaws. Unfortunately, he didn't pay attention to the overall cloudiness of the diamond and to its unusually thick rim. Consequently, Ken's girlfriend was disappointed that the diamond did not look as big and brilliant as other one-carat diamonds she had seen.

Judy's favorite pastime was shopping, particularly for jewelry. So when she saw that there was a sale on diamonds, she rushed over to the store. Although Judy was in the market for a cocktail ring instead of a solitaire, she had a hard time believing diamond rings could be so cheap because, like Ken, she had already compared the prices in other stores.

Judy had a better eye for style than many professional jewelry buyers. She picked out a diamond ring that not only had a lot of brilliance and sparkle, but also a very flattering and original design. However, Judy neglected to notice the sharp points of the ring mounting that ended up snagging several of her dresses and countless number of nylons. One night she knocked the ring against a table and badly chipped the center diamond. When she bought the ring, she hadn't noticed the long, deep crack extending across the stone.

Paul and Joyce were about to celebrate their 20th anniversary and had been looking around for a stone to replace Joyce's 1/4 carat engagement diamond. They too decided to go to the store mentioned in the solitaire ring ad. The salesman showed them a brownish-tinted diamond and claimed that due to its unique color, it was more valuable than colorless diamonds. This contradicted what another salesperson had told them.

Paul and Joyce had heard somewhere that you should judge a diamond by the four c's of color, cut, clarity, and carat weight, but it was unclear to them how these factors affected diamond prices. They were particularly confused about the term *cut* because they had heard it used in different ways. Sometimes it was used to refer to the shape or cutting style of a diamond. Other times it was used to mean how the diamond was proportioned. They never did understand how to distinguish a good cut from a poor cut.

After looking at several diamonds, Joyce and Paul were so confused about what type of diamond to buy that they decided to leave the store. As they were going out, they spotted a travel agency next door with a poster on Austria. Just then they had a bright idea. Why not spend the money they'd set aside for a diamond on a ski trip to Austria instead? They went skiing and had a great time.

After the ski trip, Joyce couldn't help but notice how small her diamond looked compared to others she had looked at. She knew she could still afford a bigger and better diamond, and she wanted another permanent reminder of her relationship with Paul. But like any intelligent buyer, she didn't want to make a purchase that she would regret later on.

Suppose Joyce had a book that explained how color and cut affect value. And suppose this book even had photos showing examples of good and bad cuts. Wouldn't it help her determine which salesperson was better informed? Wouldn't it help her select a better diamond for her price range?

Suppose Judy had a book that gave practical pointers about choosing diamond ring mountings and setting styles. Wouldn't this help her choose a ring more suitable to her needs?

Suppose Ken had a book that emphasized the importance of diamond brilliancy and explained how shape and cutting proportions can affect a diamond's sparkle, brilliancy, and apparent size. Wouldn't it help him select a ring that would make his girlfriend happier?

So often people say, "I never buy jewelry for myself or as a gift because I don't know what I'm buying." These people are smart. Why would any intelligent consumer want to be at the total mercy of a salesperson? And how can anyone appreciate something he or she knows little about?

If you glance at the table of contents of *The Diamond Ring Buying Guide*, you will notice a wide range of subjects relevant to buying a diamond ring. There is no way a brochure could cover them adequately. Likewise, it would be impossible for jewelers to discuss thoroughly subjects such as gold, platinum, setting styles, craftsmanship, etc. during a brief visit to their store. It would be better to first get a fundamental knowledge by reading this book. Jewelers can show you how to apply your new-found knowledge when selecting a ring, and they can help you find what you want.

When learning about something as important as buying diamonds, it's normal to question the credibility of your sources. I am a graduate gemologist (GIA) and my specialty is diamonds. I evaluate and identify diamonds of all sizes, shapes, and qualities which have been cut in Belgium, Israel, India, and the U.S.S.R. These diamonds in turn are sold to jewelry stores, jewelry manufacturers, or diamond dealers. I also oversee the production of diamond jewelry and am responsible for determining the cost of the material and labor involved and for then establishing the price at which this jewelry will be sold to jewelry stores. Part of my job is to examine the quality of gold and platinum mountings coming from various manufacturers and jewelers in Europe, Asia, and North America. Consequently, every day I get hands-on experience pricing and evaluating many types of diamond jewelry from a wide variety of sources. There are constantly new developments in the industry, however, and there is a variety of ways to approach the study of gems and jewelry, so differences of opinion can arise. Any comments or criticisms you might have to offer regarding the content of this book would be appreciated and may be addressed to me in care of the publisher.

What This Book Is Not

♦ A guide to making a fortune on diamonds and gold. Nobody can guarantee that diamonds and gold will increase in value and that your jewelry can be resold for more than its retail cost. However, understanding the value concepts discussed in this book can increase your chances of finding good buys on jewelry.

♦ A ten-minute guide to appraising a diamond ring. There's a lot to learn before being able to accurately compare diamonds for value. That's why a book is needed on the subject. *The Diamond Ring Buying Guide* is just an introduction, but it does have enough information to give laypeople a good background for understanding jewelry price differences.

♦ A scientific treatise for gem experts. Technical explanations and terms such as *specific gravity* and *refractive index* are intentionally avoided. However, technical terms needed for buying or for understanding diamond grading are explained in everyday language.

♦ A discussion of famous diamonds or diamond mining and cutting. Excellent books have already been written on these subjects.

♦ A catalogue of diamond rings. These can be obtained at jewelry stores.

♦ A substitute for examining actual diamonds. To understand diamond transparency, brilliancy, and color, you need to see the real stone. Diamonds are three-dimensional. Photos are two-dimensional.

What This Book Is

♦ A guide to evaluating diamond quality and jewelry craftsmanship.

♦ A collection of practical tips on choosing ring styles, setting styles, diamonds, and jewelers.

♦ A handy reference for your questions on gold, platinum, and diamonds.

♦ An aid to avoiding fraud by offering hints on detecting diamond imitations and stone switching.

♦ A challenge to view diamonds from a new perspective—through the eyes of gemologists, scientists, artists, and even diamonds themselves.

How to Use This Book

The Diamond Ring Buying Guide is not meant to be read like a murder mystery or a science fiction thriller. So much information is introduced that it would be impossible for a layperson to absorb it all in one sitting. Some people may even find that the book has more information than they care to know. It might be advisable for these people to just look through the pictures, learn the basic diamond terms defined in Chapter Three, and then read Chapter Two ("A Message from the Spokesman for the Diamond Kingdom"), Chapter Sixteen, and the Table of Contents. Then they will be in a position to use this book as a quick reference when questions and concerns arise about diamond jewelry.

For those of you who are seriously interested in diamonds and jewelry, it might be best to just read and reread a chapter or two at a time. It's not essential that the chapters be read in consecutive order, but it will be easier because references are occasionally made to material in preceding chapters. Quizzes have been included at the end of some chapters to help reinforce the concepts you've learned. Besides taking them, you should also try examining jewelry with the help of experienced jewelers, appraisers, or gemologists. If you have appraisals or grading reports on diamonds or jewelry, study them carefully. If there is something you don't understand, ask for an explanation. When you examine jewelry, keep in mind that rubies, emeralds, and other gemstones are not judged and valued in the same way as diamonds. However, knowing how to grade a diamond will make it easier for you to learn how to grade other gemstones.

Jewelry shopping should not be a chore; it should be fun. There is no fun, however, in worrying about being deceived or in buying a diamond ring that turns out to be a poor choice. Use this book to gain the knowledge, confidence, and independence needed to select the diamond ring that is best for you. Use it also to gain a greater appreciation for the jewelry you already own. Buying a diamond ring represents a significant investment of time and money. Let *The Diamond Ring Buying Guide* help make this investment a pleasurable and rewarding experience.

2

The Diamond—Just Another Rock?

A Message From the Spokesman for the Diamond Kingdom

We diamonds have a couple confessions to make. We are not natural beauties and we are not forever.

Yes, it's true. When people see us lying in a stream or in a pile of dirt, they usually think we're just another rock. We look so ordinary. The first person that picked us up never dreamed we could both serve him and dazzle him. As time passed by, his descendants learned that we could cut any kind of rock or metal, but nothing could cut us except another diamond, so naturally we got drafted as saws, knives, and drills. Yes, diamonds were used as tools long before they were cut as jewels.

We're proud of the Taj Majal in India. Its intricate marble designs were cut by diamond tools. We're equally proud to see how indispensable we are to twentieth-century man. He uses us to drill for oil and gas, to mine ores, to fashion gemstones, to cut metal parts for cars, rockets, and farm machinery. Dentists use us to drill teeth. Surgeons use us to cut bone and tissue.

When man discovered that we diamonds can drill and cut better than anything else, he only began to recognize our potential. Outer space and defense programs now take advantage of our ability to resist radiation, temperature, and chemical damage. The electronics industry relies on us because not only can we conduct heat as well as any metal, we are also good electrical insulators. Think of us the next time you use a phone, a computer, a refrigerator, a television, or an electric light. Is it any wonder that General Electric and Japan's Sumitomo Electric Industries have spent so much time and money learning to create diamonds? Yes, man-made diamonds are now a reality.

17

Most of you people are probably more familiar with our optical qualities--our transparency, brilliance, and sparkle. These have not only earned us a reputation as the most important gemstone, they have also increased our practical value by making us useful for lenses, lasers, and windows for outer space.

Maybe you think we're conceited for telling you how good we are. We're only trying to prove that we're not just another rock. Actually, we'd be the first to admit that we're only simple folk. Coal and pencil lead are our next of kin. All of us are nothing but carbon, and that's why you can't say that diamonds are forever. When you heat us in oxygen up to about 700° C (1292° F), we start turning to carbon dioxide or carbon monoxide.

We can understand, though, that someone who has a hard time making it past the age of 100 would think that a diamond that's a few million years old is forever; but to us, a few million years isn't much. Your scientists are finally beginning to realize that we existed long before your solar system did, now that they're studying us in meteorites.

Man also has a hard time imagining that something so simple and practical as a diamond can be transformed into a handsome work of art. Maybe that's why it took him so long to bring out our inner beauty. It's only been in the last few hundred years that he's cut tiny geometrical windows around us to reflect and let in light. Until about 1919, most of us looked a bit lackluster compared to the way we look today. Then the mathematician Marcel Tolkowsky published a complex formula for cutting us that made us more brilliant.

The Tolkowsky formula and other similar ones can only work well on diamonds that pass the jewel qualifying exam--an inspection so severe that about 75% of all diamonds fail. This exam is a nightmare for us. The results determine whether we will bask under someone's appreciative eye or slave away as, perhaps, a drill.

After we've qualified as potential jewels, we undergo a beauty makeover that transforms us from ordinary looking rocks into extraordinary looking jewels. Makeover artists, also called diamond cutters, are in charge of this process. When they are finished, we start entering beauty contests. To get top scores in these contests, diamonds must have a lively and sparkling personality, an attractive shape, a clean character, and individual charm. The judging is subjective and often there are hot debates over the scoring, particularly when large sums of prize money are at stake.

You might expect that the winners of these beauty contests have the best lives. More often than not they end up stuck in a safe deposit box, especially the large diamonds. It's true that life as a drill is a real bore, but life in a dark lonely box is not much better. Occasionally, some of the winners end up in museums and have a pretty good life, but those diamonds that end up the happiest are those worn day in and day out by you. Yet these are not normally the diamonds with the highest scores.

I suspect you find it strange that I talk about diamonds being happy. Plato and other great philosophers knew that we diamonds are living beings and have the same types of feelings as humans, but for some reason, most of you don't want to accept this fact. Let me assure you that we diamonds do have feelings, both positive and negative.

We are angered and hurt when people are duped into losing their life savings on us, when workers in the diamond industry are exploited, when arguments, robberies, murders, and wars occur because of us. Somebody even told us that we were part of the cause of the French revolution. It had something to do with a diamond necklace scandal. But, on second thought, maybe our role in that scandal was more positive than negative. When terrible things happen because of us, blame yourselves for misusing diamonds, don't blame us.

Fortunately life is not all bad; we do a lot of good. We create jobs for hundreds of thousands of people. We give people a means of escaping from oppressive governments. Non-jewel diamonds help supply you with food, energy, transportation, medical equipment, and comfortable homes.

All of this good gives us great satisfaction, but there is something that gives us even more pleasure. It's when our mere presence makes man happy. What a joy it is to see the delight in the eye of newlyweds admiring their diamond wedding rings. What a joy it is to see a widow's grief interrupted by memories of some of the happiest moments of her life, as she looks down at her diamond engagement ring. What a joy it is to see people momentarily forget their everyday worries and frustrations and focus on thoughts of beauty and love, as they glance at us on their hands or wrists.

As long as you enjoy us and use us toward good ends, we diamonds don't expect anything in return for brightening up your lives. Well, maybe that's a bit of a lie. We will be bold enough to ask one little favor of you. It's this: If anyone ever tries to tell you that the diamond is just another rock, please tell him he's full of poppycock.

3

Diamond Shapes and Cutting Styles

The shape of a diamond not only affects how big and brilliant it looks, but it may even reveal personality traits of the buyer.

Saul Spero, a New York diamond appraiser and gem consultant, spent twenty-five years interviewing over 50,000 people and developing a system of predicting personality types mainly based on a person's first three preferences of diamond shapes. In his book *Diamonds, Love, & Compatibility*, Spero discusses the six basic shapes seen in figures 3.1 to 3.6. He states that if a woman has an exclusive preference for any of these shaped diamonds, she could be characterized as follows:

Exclusive Preference for

Round	Home- and family-centered, dependable, unaggressive, easy to get along with, and security conscious.
Oval	Individualistic, creative, well-organized, dependable, willing to take chances.
Pear	Conforming, considerate, adaptable, home- and community-centered.
Heart	Sentimental, creative, feminine, sensitive, trusting, dramatic, a dreamer.
Marquise	Extroverted, aggressive, experimental, exciting, innovative, career-centered.
Rectangle or Square	Disciplined, organized, conservative, efficient, honest and open.

Fig. 3.1 Round

Fig. 3.2 Oval

Fig. 3.3 Pear shape

Fig. 3.4 Heart shape

Fig. 3.5 Marquise

Fig. 3.6 Rectangular emerald cut

Please note that the above personality profiles are for women who like only one shape. Most women like more than one diamond shape which is why Spero also evaluated personality types in terms of their second and third choices. A more complete discussion on diamond shape and personality supported by examples can be found in Spero's book.

There are more than the six above-mentioned shapes to choose from. Triangular shapes are becoming increasingly popular. You can also find stars, horses heads, Christmas trees, fish, fruit, boats, and letters of the alphabet (figs. 3.7 to 3.10). Some people even have diamonds cut in the form of their state, province, or country. The possibilities are limitless.

Diamond Terms Defined

Before you can thoroughly understand a discussion of diamond shapes and styles, some terminology must be explained. Some basic terms are as follows:

Facets	The flat, polished surfaces or planes on a diamond.
Table	The large, flat, top facet. It has an octagonal shape on a round brilliant diamond.
Girdle	The narrow rim around the diamond. The girdle plane is parallel to the table and is the largest diameter of any part of the stone.
Crown	The upper part of the diamond above the girdle.
Pavilion	The lower part of the diamond below the girdle. It's cone-shaped on a round diamond.
Culet	The tiny facet on the pointed bottom of the pavilion, parallel to the table.
Brilliant Cut	The most common style of diamond cutting. The standard brilliant cut consists of 32 facets plus a table above the girdle and 24 facets plus a culet below the girdle (fig. 3.12).
Bezel Facets	Kite-shape facets on the crown of brilliant-cut diamonds. The star, pavilion mains, and upper and lower girdle facets are other facets found on brilliant cuts (fig. 3.12).
Fancies or Fancy Shapes	Any shape except round. A pear shape is an example of a fancy shape.

Figs. 3.7 to 3.10. Fantasy-cut diamonds, trademarked **"SCULPTAIRES."** The diamonds represent a pineapple, a boat, the letter "A" and a 0.99 ct fish in a porthole. Photos and diamonds are courtesy Global Diamonds, Inc., Chicago.

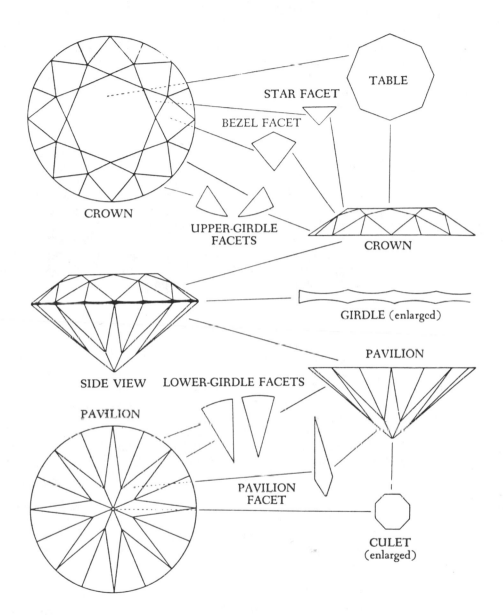

Fig. 3.12 Facet arrangement of a standard round brilliant cut. Diagram courtesy of the GIA.

Cutting Styles

The two concepts of shape and cutting style are often described by one term in the jewelry trade. For example, when a jeweler uses the term **baguette**, he's referring to a square-cornered, rectangular-shaped diamond with rows of step-like facets (fig. 3.13). If the two long sides of the baguette taper inward, it is called a **tapered baguette** (fig. 3.15). An **emerald cut** is a rectangular stone with step-like facets that looks like its corners were clipped off (fig. 3.6). Usually emerald cuts have more facets or steps than baguettes.

The GIA (Gemological Institute of America) has simplified the description of cutting styles by limiting them to three basic types:

Step Cut Has rows of facets that resemble the steps of a staircase and are usually four-sided and elongated. The emerald and baguette cuts are examples of the step cut. Sometimes the term *emerald cut* is used as a synonym for *step cut*. For example, jewelers sometimes ask for an emerald-cut triangle, meaning step-cut triangle (fig. 3.14). Normally, an emerald cut is rectangular or square. The step cut is frequently used for colored transparent gemstones.

Brilliant Cut Has triangular-, kite-, or lozenge-shaped facets that radiate outward around the stone. Examples of these are the pear, oval, heart, and marquise (figs. 3.2 - 3.5) and the standard round brilliant (figs 3.1 & 3.7). Three other modifications of the brilliant-cut style are the **old mine cut**, the **old European cut** (fig 3.16), and the **single cut** (fig. 3.17). The **old mine** and **old European cuts**, often seen in antique jewelry, have 58 facets and are characterized by a high crown, a small table, and a large culet. Old mine cuts, however, are squarish, whereas old European cuts are round. The **single cut**, which has 17 or 18 facets, is used on very small diamonds. The jewelry trade generally refers to round diamonds with 18 facets as **single cuts** and to those with 58 facets as **full cuts**.

Mixed Cut Has both step- and brilliant-cut facets. The pavilion, for example, can be step cut and the crown can be brilliant cut, but the step- and brilliant-cut facets can also be scattered over the diamond. This cut is occasionally used on diamonds and often used on colored transparent gemstones.

When you shop for diamonds, you probably won't hear the salespeople talk about step cuts or mixed cuts. You will, however, hear them talk about brilliant cuts and emerald cuts. They may also tell you about Radiants, Trillions, trilliants, Quadrillions, and princess cuts-- styles which have been introduced within about the last twenty-five years. To better understand what they're talking about, you can refer to the following descriptions and photos:

Fig. 3.13 Baguette

Fig. 3.14 Emerald-cut (step-cut) triangle

Fig.15 Tapered baguette

Fig. 3.16 Old European cut

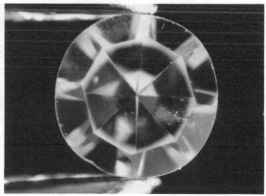

Fig. 3.17 Single cut

Radiant A rectangular- or square-shaped diamond with 70 facets cut in the brilliant style (fig. 3.18). It was designed and patented by Mr. Henry Grossbard of New York and is marketed by the I. Starck Co., Inc. of Chicago. It was first introduced in Hong Kong in 1976. A square or rectangular diamond cut in this style can display almost as much brilliance as a round, full-cut diamond.

Trielle A triangular-shaped diamond with 50 facets that are precision cut in the brilliant style. It was developed in the 1950's by Leon Finker and patented in 1978 under the name of L.F. Industries in New York. Due to their unusually large surface area, a 1-carat Trielle can look as large as a 1 1/2-carat round diamond. They have the added advantage of being easy to match because of their symmetrical sides and consistent proportions. Prior to 1991, the patented brand name for the Trielle was the **Trillion**.

Trilliant Resembles the Trielle but is often cut to retain as much weight as possible from the original diamond crystal. The facet arrangement and proportions may vary from one trilliant to another. Figure 3.19 is an example of a well-cut trilliant.

Quadrillion A square-shaped diamond with 49 facets that are precision cut in the brilliant style with a raised star pattern on the pavilion (figs. 3.20 & 3.21). It was patented and trademarked by Ambar Diamonds of Los Angeles in 1981. Quadrillions are usually channel set, creating a solid line of brilliance along a mounting.

Princess Cut Resembles the Quadrillion but is not cut to the same quality standards. It is usually cut to save as much weight as possible of the original diamond crystal in order to lower the per carat cost. Consequently, it may have a high crown, thick girdle, or bulging pavilion (Chapter Seven explains these cutting deviations). The princess cut is also called the multi-faceted square diamond or the square brilliant cut, especially when used in men's jewelry. (It looks similar to figures 3.20 & 3.21).

The Effect of Shape on Diamond Prices

The shape of a diamond can play an important role in determining its price. For example, a small, 0.07-carat square diamond may cost up to 15% more than a round diamond of the same weight, color, and quality. On the other hand, a one-carat round diamond can cost up to 20% more than a one-carat square diamond of the same color and quality. To better understand the effect of shape on diamond prices, you can refer to the following chart. In it is a comparison of the price relationship of round diamonds to fancy shapes (non-rounds) in three different carat weight categories. Assume that they are the same color and quality.

Fig. 3.18 Radiant

Fig. 3.19 Trilliant

Fig. 3.20 Quadrillion, face up

Fig. 3.21 Quadrillion, pavilion side up

Carat Weight	Fancy Shapes Cost compared to rounds	Rounds Cost compared to fancies
0.00 to 0.14 ct	sometimes more	sometimes less
0.15 to 0.29 ct	similar	similar
0.30 ct +	usually less, except for marquise shapes, which can cost the same or more	usually more

Perhaps you are wondering why round and fancy-shape diamonds are priced differently. There are a variety of reasons. Small rounds are sometimes priced lower than fancy shapes because of lower inventory and labor costs. (The additional labor cost of small fancies is partially due to the specialized skills needed to cut them). Small rounds sell more quickly so less of a profit margin is needed to cover the cost of keeping them in inventory. It's less time consuming to cut, measure, and select small rounds than small fancy shapes. Consequently, labor costs can be lower. During 1990 and 1991, however, the price differential between small round and fancy-shape diamonds decreased--to the point where both were often priced about the same.

The higher cost of round diamonds 1/4 carat and up is the result of a limited supply and a large demand. Inventory costs for rounds can be just as high as for fancy shapes because there are fewer buyers in the market for larger, more expensive diamonds.

The shape of a rough diamond crystal before it is cut also plays a role in diamond pricing. When long diamond crystals are cut into ovals, pears, and emerald cuts, they weigh more than if they had been cut into rounds. This means the per carat cost of the fancy shape can be lower than a round and still bring the same amount of profit from the original rough diamond.

Marquise diamonds are currently an exception to the above generalizations. Their cost has risen to levels equal to and higher than that of round diamonds because of a very high demand and low supply. In the United States, there is an unusually large number of requests for lower- and medium-quality marquise diamonds. Consequently, these grades of marquises often exceed the cost of rounds. Based on the history of marquise prices, if demand for them drops, their prices will also drop.

Whether a diamond is an emerald cut or a square or rectangular brilliant cut seems to have little effect on prices. Therefore, you can expect, for example, a Quadrillion to be priced like a square emerald cut of the same quality .

Judging Shape

Diamond prices are not only affected by the shape type (i.e. pear, marquise, round etc.), they are also affected by the attractiveness of the chosen shape. For example, an unsymmetrical or a long and skinny marquise diamond cannot command the same price as a well-shaped marquise.

The following diagrams show desirable shape outlines of five basic shapes. A knowledge of the ideal round shape is assumed.

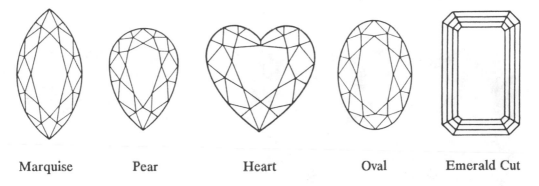

| Marquise | Pear | Heart | Oval | Emerald Cut |

(Diagrams courtesy of the Gemological Institute of America)

Let's look at some diamonds with shape outlines that do not conform to industry standards.

Note how wide the pear shape in figure 3.22 is. There is nothing intrinsically wrong with this stone. In fact, it could flatter a long, slender hand. The jewelry industry, however, places a greater value on a pear with a more traditional shape.

Note how long and skinny the diamond in figure 3.23 is. Even though it is priced less than a more traditional pear-shape stone, it could be very flattering on someone with a broad hand.

Note how the diamond in figure 3.24 looks more like a shield than a pear-shape. Some people prefer this shape, so this is best for them. But normally, stones having another shape than intended should cost a little less.

If you cut the diamond in figure 3.25 in half, the shape of the two parts would not be equal. Even though many people like free forms, symmetrical stones usually are more valued.

If you are buying a diamond for your own personal pleasure, its shape doesn't matter, as long as you like it. However, if you are buying your diamond mainly as an investment, you would be wise to select a shape conforming to industry ideals. Such shapes are often sold at premium prices and might be hard to find.

You may be wondering why all diamonds are not cut to industry standards since they would be worth more. It's because too much of the original diamond rough would be lost if it were always cut away to form standard diamond shapes. So if the diamond rough is elongated, one can expect the cutter to fashion an elongated diamond. Buyers have different tastes, too, and many of them prefer non-traditional shapes, particularly, if they can buy them at a lower price per carat.

What Shape Diamond is Best for You?

To answer this question, let's consider some of the factors that will determine what shape diamond is best for you.

♦ **Your personal preference.** This should play the greatest role in your choice. There is no point in wearing a diamond if you don't like its looks. However, most people like more than one shape. Therefore it's helpful for them to know how the various shapes affect a diamond's brilliance, apparent size, and price.

♦ **The amount of brilliance and sparkle you want your diamond to display.** The shape and cutting style that shows the most brilliance and sparkle is the round brilliant. This is probably the single biggest reason why round diamonds under three carats are more popular than any other shape.
   Emerald cuts have less sparkle than brilliant cuts, but many people like their sleek, elegant look. People who would prefer a rectangular or square diamond with more sparkle can buy a Quadrillion or Radiant Cut.
   Even though fancy shapes are normally not as brilliant as rounds, when they are cut properly, they can display a great deal of brilliance. There are more factors than just shape and cutting style which influence the brilliance of a diamond. Chapter Seven will explain these in more detail.

♦ **How much you want your diamond to weigh.** In sizes over three carats, fancy-shape diamonds often outsell round diamonds. This is because many people think that large, fancy-shape diamonds look more elegant and less pretentious than large round ones. If you are buying a big diamond, see how the various shaped diamonds look on your hand. Then make your choice.

♦ **How big you want your diamond to look.** A lot of people want their diamond to look as big as possible, even if it doesn't weigh much. Fancy shapes generally look bigger than round diamonds of equal weight, particularly if they are elongated like the marquise and pear. The Trielle is also known for looking bigger than it weighs. The people that market it claim that it looks nearly 50% larger than a round brilliant diamond of the same weight because it is cut wide and shallow.

♦ **The shape and size of your hand.** The shape of your diamond can give the illusion that your hand looks longer or shorter than it is. For example, a long, thin diamond set lengthwise along your finger can make your hand look longer and thinner. A broad diamond or long one set horizontally across your finger can make your hand look broader and shorter. Try on a few shapes and see which one flatters your hand the most.

♦ **The color and clarity of the diamond** (how flawed it is). The shape and cutting style that can best mask flaws and yellow tints is the round brilliant. In emerald cuts and baguettes, the flaws become the most obvious. What this means is that a low quality, less expensive, round brilliant can look very good to the naked eye, whereas a step-cut, rectangular or triangular diamond of the same quality might look unacceptable.

♦ **The availability of the shapes.** Even if you like a specific shape, you may find that there is a very poor selection in the size or quality you want to buy. For example, you might have a hard time finding a well-shaped one-carat marquise and end up buying another shape instead. If you have your heart set on a specific shape, ask your jeweler to find it for you. He can call around to various diamond dealers until he finds the diamond that meets your needs, but be prepared to give him the time he needs to find your stone.

♦ **Your purpose for buying the diamond--pleasure or investment**. If you're buying a diamond for personal pleasure, any shape you like can be a good choice. But if resale for profit is your goal, you need to consider what shapes are most in demand and are likely to stay in demand. If the diamond is less than three carats in weight, you are more likely to find a buyer for a round diamond. For stones over three carats, you will probably find it hard to find an immediate buyer no matter what shape you buy, mainly because so few people can afford investment quality diamonds that size. However, fancy shapes might be a better choice for stones over three carats since they outsell large round diamonds.

To simplify this discussion on choosing a diamond shape, we have only considered diamond solitaires. For those interested in cocktail rings, anniversary bands, or any ring with many small diamonds, the following table may be helpful. It compares the advantages of round brilliants to those of fancy shapes weighing less than 0.09 carat.

Round Brilliants (<0.09 ct)	Fancy Shapes (<0.09 ct)
More brilliance	Less brilliance than well-cut rounds
Sometimes less expensive	Sometimes more expensive
Easier to replace	Harder to replace
Easier to match	Harder to match
Flaws less visible	Flaws more visible, especially in step cuts
Easier to set	Harder to set
Lower setting costs	Higher setting costs, especially for square and rectangular stones

This table is a bit misleading because it gives the impression there are no advantages to buying small fancies when, in fact, there are. Fancy shape diamonds make possible a wider selection of ring designs. Furthermore, they can enhance large center stones and add stylistic effects not possible with rounds. Baguettes surrounding a green emerald compliment it. They don't outdazzle it or compete with it the way a cluster of round diamonds might.

The above table is also over-simplified. For example, it does not point out that tapered baguettes cost more than straight baguettes, but you don't need to be concerned with details. Just be aware that rings with small fancies cost more and require more labor than those with small round brilliants. This will help you realize the importance of comparing rings having diamonds of the same shape as well as the same size, color, and clarity. Then, you will be able to judge value more accurately.

4

Carat Weight

Which sounds more impressive?

♦ *One-carat diamond*

♦ *Diamond weighing one-fifth of a gram*

♦ *200-milligram diamond*

All three diamonds are the same weight. So if you thought *one-carat diamond*, sounds more impressive, then you can understand why the jewelry industry prefers to use *carats* instead of *grams* to express gemstone weight. The term *carat* originated in ancient times when gemstones were weighed against the carob bean. Each bean weighed about one carat. In 1913, carat weight was standardized internationally and adapted to the metric system.

The weight of small diamonds is frequently expressed in points, with one point equaling 0.01 carats. For example, five points is a short way of saying five one-hundredths of a carat. Diamonds weighing 0.05 ct are referred to as five pointers. Examine the following written and spoken forms of carat weight:

Written	Spoken
0.005 ct (0.5 pt.)	half point
0.05 ct	five points
0.25 ct	twenty-five points or quarter carat
0.50 ct	fifty points or half carat
1.82 cts.	one point eight two (carats) or one eighty-two

Note that *point* when used in expressing weights over one carat refers to the decimal point, not a unit of measure. Also note that *pt* can be used instead of *ct* to make people think their diamond is 100 times heavier than it is.

Effect of Carat Weight on Price

Most people are familiar with the principle, the higher the carat weight the greater the diamond value. However, in actual practice, this principle is more complicated than it appears. This can be illustrated by having you arrange the following four rings in the order of decreasing diamond value. Assume that the quality, shape, and color of all the diamonds are the same.

    a. 1 carat diamond solitaire ring (one diamond only)
    b. 1 carat TW, 24 diamond wedding ring
    c. 2 carat diamond solitaire ring
    d. 2 carat TW, 48 diamond wedding ring

In almost all cases, the order of decreasing value would be c>a>d>b. In rare cases, the order might be c>d>a>b. Strangely enough, a single one-carat diamond usually costs more than two carats of small diamonds of the same quality. This is because the supply of larger diamonds is very limited. So when you compare ring prices, you should pay attention to individual diamond weights and **notice the difference between** the labels **1 ct TW** (one carat total weight) **and 1 ct** (the weight of one stone). A ring with a **1 ct**, colorless, top quality diamond can be worth more than 10 times as much as a ring with **1 ct TW** diamonds of the same quality.

When comparing diamond cost, you should also start noting the **per carat cost** instead of concentrating on the stone cost or the total diamond cost. To understand why, try comparing the cost of the following three diamonds. Assume they are the same color, shape, and quality.

Weight	Total Stone Cost
1.00 ct	$6,000
1.20 ct	$7,080
1.30 ct	$7,540

Most people find it hard to determine the best value just by looking at the total stone cost. Now try to compare values by looking at the per carat cost of the same diamonds.

Weight	Per Carat Cost
1.00 ct	$6.000
1.20 ct	$5,900
1.30 ct	$5,800

Normally, the 1.30 ct diamond should cost the same or more per carat than the other two stones. However, in this case, it costs less. Consequently, the 1.30 ct stone is the best buy. But it's only when we compare the per carat prices of the stones that this becomes evident. Therefore **when you shop for diamonds, think in terms of the per carat cost.** This is what diamond dealers do. To calculate the per carat cost or the total cost of a diamond, use the following equations:

$$\textbf{Per carat cost} = \frac{\textbf{stone cost}}{\textbf{carat weight}}$$

Total cost of a stone = carat weight x per carat cost

It is not enough to know that the weight and per carat costs of diamonds are very important factors for comparing the value of diamond rings. You need details on how carat weight affects price. Let's first compare round diamonds. Their per carat price usually increases by about 5% to 50% as they move up from one weight category to another. Usually this increase is lower for poorer quality diamonds. These categories can vary from one dealer to another but may be outlined as follows:

Weight Categories for Diamonds	
0.00 ct — 0.08 ct	0.50 ct — 0.69 ct
0.09 ct — 0.14 ct	0.70 ct — 0.89 ct
0.15 ct — 0.17 ct	0.90 ct — 0.95 ct
0.18 ct — 0.22 ct	0.96 ct — 0.99 ct
0.23 ct — 0.29 ct	1.00 ct — 1.49 ct
0.30 ct — 0.37 ct	1.50 ct — 2.00 ct
0.38 ct — 0.45 ct	2.00 ct — 2.50 ct
0.46 ct — 0.49 ct	2.50 ct — 3.00 ct

(The above categories and the 5% to 50% percentage increase estimate are based mainly on the *Rapaport Diamond Report*, a price guide for wholesalers).

The list of weight categories tells you, for example, that the per carat price of two round diamonds each weighing from 0.50 ct to 0.69 ct should be about the same if their quality is the same. A 3/4 carat diamond would cost 5% to 50% more per carat than a diamond weighing 0.60 carat.

There are a couple of important exceptions to the rule that as diamond weight increases, per carat value increases. Because of high demand, diamonds weighing 5, 10, or 15 points can cost more per carat than larger odd-size diamonds. Also better quality .01 ct to .035 ct diamonds sometimes cost more per carat than diamonds weighing from .06 ct to .08 ct. Occasionally, diamonds as large as 13 points cost less per carat than 3 point diamonds of the same quality. This was sometimes the case during 1987-89, when there was an unusually high demand for three pointers for tennis bracelets.

You may think it easier just to be given a diamond price list instead of listing weight categories and explaining the system of how diamonds are priced. However, if you understand the system, you will find it easier to interpret price guides and compare diamond ring values. The system of diamond pricing changes very slowly, but price guides can change weekly. During a one-week period in 1988, for example, USA dollar prices for diamond increased about 13% but the system of charging more per carat for greater stone weight remained the same. Small standard sizes and 1 to 3 point diamonds were still sold at premium prices. Therefore, this book will concentrate on the system of diamond pricing and avoid listing diamond prices. Otherwise, it would be obsolete the moment it is published.

So far, this chapter has only discussed the per carat prices of round stones. Small fancy shapes (non-round diamonds less than 0.15 ct) do not fit into the same weight categories as small round diamonds. They sometimes cost more per carat than round stones. In larger sizes (more than 0.29 ct), fancy shapes fit into the same weight categories as round diamonds, but they cost less per carat. The exception to this rule is the lower- and mid-quality marquise shape which currently is worth more or about the same per carat as a round diamond of the same quality. This is due to a high demand for this quality marquise, especially in the United States.

Now look at the list of the following four diamond rings, which are the same color and quality. Are they arranged in the order of their decreasing diamond value? If not, put them in the correct order.

   a. 1 ct round diamond solitaire ring
   b. 1 ct emerald-cut diamond solitaire ring
   c. 1 ct TW ring with 15 baguette (rectangular) diamonds
   d. 1 ct TW ring with 15 round diamonds

If you left them as is, you are correct Small baguettes tend to cost more per carat than small rounds. And large round diamonds cost more than large emerald cuts or baguettes. Small rounds are considerably less per carat than large rounds.

The complexity of diamond pricing can be discouraging, but you don't need to know the details of the system to shop for value. Just be aware that shape and carat weight can affect the per carat value of diamonds and follow these two guidelines:

♦ Compare per carat weight instead of total weight.

♦ When judging prices, compare diamonds of the same size, shape, quality, and color.

Size Versus Carat Weight

Sometimes in the jewelry trade, the term *size* is used as a synonym for *carat weight*. This is because small round diamonds having the same weight also look the same size and have similar diameters. As diamonds increase in weight, their size becomes less predictable. This means that a 0.90 carat diamond can look bigger than a 1.00 carat diamond. So if you want a bigger looking diamond, you need to consider diamond measurements as well as carat weight. This doesn't mean that you need to carry a millimeter gauge with you when you go shopping. It just means that you should start noting the different illusions of size that different diamond shapes and measurements can create.

You should also note that diamonds usually have different measurements than other gemstones having the same weight. For example because of its high density, a one-carat cubic zirconia is considerably smaller than a one-carat diamond. On the other hand, a one-carat emerald, due to its lower density, is bigger than a one-carat diamond.

Estimating Carat Weight

If you buy a diamond ring in a reputable jewelry store, you normally don't need to know how to estimate the carat weight of the diamonds because the weight will be marked on the ring. However, if you buy diamond jewelry at flea markets or auctions, it is to your advantage to know how to roughly estimate weight.

Probably the easiest way to estimate weight is to carry a diamond weight estimator with you. It's an inexpensive piece of metal or plastic that has cutouts or diagrams of diamond sizes corresponding to various diamond weights (figs. 4.1 and 4.2). They can be found in jewelry supply stores. Remember that since these estimators do not take into consideration the depth of a diamond or its girdle thickness, they can only give a general idea of the weight. Jewelry supply stores also sell gauges that measure diamond depth, but they are more expensive and more complicated to use.

Another way of getting a general idea of the weight of the diamond is to measure the diameter with a fine ruler and compare it with diameters listed on weight estimation charts such as the one on the following page. Remember, diameter measurements can be misleading. The only accurate way of determining the weight of a diamond is to take it out of its setting and weigh it. This, however, is not always possible nor advisable.

Approximate Diameters of Round, Full-cut Diamonds and Their Corresponding Weights		
Weight in Carats	Diameter in Millimeters	Diameter in Inches (Approximate)
0.01 ct	1.3 mm	1/20"
0.03 ct	2.0 mm	
0.05 ct	2.4 mm	1/10"
0.10 ct	3.0 mm	1/8"
0.15 ct	3.4 mm	
0.20 ct	3.8 mm	
0.25 ct	4.1 mm	1/6"
0.33 ct	4.4 mm	
0.50 ct	5.1 mm	1/5"
0.75 ct	5.9 mm	
1.00 ct	6.5 mm	1/4"
1.50 ct	7.4 mm	
2.00 ct	8.2 mm	1/3"
8.00 ct	13.0 mm	1/2"

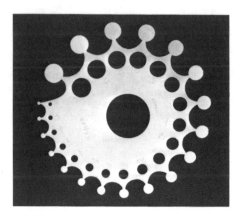

Fig. 4.1 Metal weight estimator

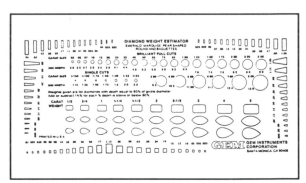

Fig. 4.2 Clear plastic diamond weight estimator

Chapter Four Quiz

For each of the following pairs of rings, select the ring that would normally be worth the most **in terms of diamond value**. Assume that the total diamond weight of each ring is one carat and that the color and quality of all the diamonds are the same.

1.   2.

    a.   b.   a.   b.

3.   4.

    a.   b.   a.   b.

5. Is it possible for a 0.95 carat diamond to look bigger than a 1.05 carat diamond? Explain your answer.

6. What's a ten-pointer diamond?

7. When could a one-carat cubic zirconia and a one-carat diamond have the same measurements?

8. If a two-carat diamond costs $8000, how much does it cost per carat?

9. How much does a 1/4 carat diamond cost if it sells for $1000 per carat?

10. Does a round-brilliant, one-carat diamond always have a diameter of 6.5 mm?

Answers

1. a. Large fancy shapes normally cost less than rounds of the same weight and quality.

2. a. The marquise normally has a higher per carat cost than other large fancy shapes. Sometimes it's even priced higher than large rounds.

3. a. A one-carat diamond will cost more per carat than a 1/4 carat diamond of the same shape and quality.

4. a. Small baguettes normally cost more per carat than small rounds of the same quality.

5. Yes. A 0.95 carat round diamond with a thin girdle can look bigger than a 1.05 carat round diamond with an extremely thick girdle and a high crown. A 0.95 carat Trillion generally looks bigger than a 1.05 carat round diamond.

6. A diamond that weighs 0.10 ct (1/10 of a carat).

7. Never, because of the diamond's lower density.

8. $4000 $$\frac{\$8000}{2 \text{ ct}} = \$4000$$

9. $250 $$1/4 \times \$1000 = \$250$$

10. No. Its diameter will vary according to its proportions. 6.5 mm represents an average diameter for well-cut, round-brilliant diamonds weighing one carat.

5

Diamond Color

On April 28, 1987, a 0.95 carat diamond was sold for $880,000 at Christie's in New York. It contained two large flaws, one of which was a deep cavity in the table (top center facet) of the diamond. Despite its flaws and small size, it set a new world record per carat price for any gem sold at auction: $926,000 (reported by the summer 1987 issue of *Gems and Gemology*).

Why did that diamond command such a high price? Because its natural color was an extremely rare, deep, purplish-red. Color plays a significant role in determining the price of a diamond.

Many people are surprised to learn that diamonds come in a wide variety of colors including green, orange, yellow, blue, brown, and black. But such diamonds are not very common, so they have been given a special name--**fancy color diamonds**, meaning diamonds with a natural body color other than light yellow, light brown, or light gray.

What color diamond, then, is best? That's a matter of personal opinion. What color diamond is most expensive? Currently the answer is purplish red; but natural green, purple, and deep blue are also unusually expensive. You're probably more familiar with non-fancy diamonds, the ones that don't show much color. The most expensive diamonds in this category are those that are colorless.

When you look at diamonds in the jewelry stores, they may all seem colorless. But if you look closely, you will notice that they normally have slight tints of yellow, gray, or brown. The strength of these tints partially determines the price of the diamond. The more the tint the lower the price, just the opposite of fancy color diamonds. To best understand the effect of these tints on diamond prices, you need to know how diamond color is categorized in both small and large diamonds. First let's discuss the broad color categories of small (1/4 carat or less) non-fancy color diamonds.

Color Categories of Small Diamonds

These categories are arranged below from the most expensive to the least expensive. Supply and demand are the main determinants of the price structure.

Colorless (also called exceptional white or **collection**). Completely colorless diamonds are so rare and expensive that jewelers will seldom use them for their regular inventory pieces. Often these diamonds are reserved for custom-made jewelry.

Near colorless (also called **white**). This is the second most expensive color group for diamonds. When these diamonds are mounted in jewelry, even expert graders may find it difficult or impossible to distinguish them from colorless diamonds. Fine quality stores usually have some jewelry with white diamonds in their inventory. Discount stores generally can't afford to use these diamonds in their jewelry.

Faint yellow (also called **top silver**). Diamonds with a tinge of yellow are fairly common. Consequently, they are less expensive than colorless diamonds and often used in discount jewelry. This does not mean they are inferior. Some people prefer a yellow tint because it conveys a feeling of warmth or because it might look good with their skin color. Fine quality jewelry stores also use these diamonds in their jewelry in order to meet the needs of all their clientele.

In order to see the difference between colorless and faint yellow diamonds when they are mounted in jewelry, you will probably have to put jewelry pieces with the two qualities side by side. The yellowish diamonds will blend in more with the gold and the colorless diamonds will provide more of a contrast and probably look brighter.

Light brown (also called **brownies**). Brownish tinted diamonds are the least expensive color of diamonds used for jewelry. If diamond rings are being promoted at unusually low prices, there is a good chance that brownish goods have been used. This does not mean that these rings are of inferior quality. It only means that the store can afford to offer them at a lower price because it paid less (probably 30% to 50% less) for brownish diamonds than for white diamonds. One promotional term for brownish tinted diamonds is **champagne diamonds**.

Color Categories of Larger Diamonds

The broad color categories used for small diamonds are divided into more precise categories when grading larger diamonds, particularly those weighing over 1/3 carat. The most widely used color grading system is the one developed by the GIA (Gemological Institute of America), which identifies colors with alphabetical letters ranging from D to Z+. It is so well-known throughout the world that even if your jeweler uses another system, he should know how to translate his grades into GIA grades. The diagram below shows how this system relates to the one used for grading smaller diamonds.

D E F*	G H I J	K L M	N to Z	Z +
colorless	near colorless	faint yellow	very light or	fancy
(collection)	(white)	(top silver)	light yellow	yellow

(*Colorless for 0.50 ct or less, near colorless for heavier stones)

In terms of price, D (no color) is the most expensive color and N through Z (the darker colors) the least expensive. Diamonds yellow enough to be classified as fancies are not priced in this way. Their price increases as the intensity of their color increases.

Light brown diamonds can also be assigned letter grades according to their depth of color. Brownish tints in large diamonds tend to reduce their value just as they do in small sizes.

North American students hate to receive grades in school of D or F. Jewelers love it when their diamonds receive a D, E, or F grade from a gem laboratory since these represent the most expensive diamond color grades. The difference between a D and an F stone is basically a matter of transparency with D being the most transparent. Because of their rarity, it is not easy to find D, E, and F color diamonds. Your jeweler may even have to call around the country to find one in the size, shape, and quality you want.

If your diamond has a G to I or even J color grade, you should be very pleased because such diamonds can be worth a lot of money. The average consumer doesn't even notice yellow tints in mounted diamonds having a grade from D to J because the increasing nuances of color are so slight. The yellow color of diamonds with a grade of N to Z is noticeable and you should expect to pay considerably less for these diamonds. For example, a Q color stone could cost up to ten times less than a D color stone of the same size and quality.

How to Color Grade

Probably the best way to learn to color grade is to ask your jeweler to show you how. He will have some loose diamonds, a paper or plastic white grading tray, possibly a set of graded comparison diamonds called master stones, and a good light source such as a cool white, filtered, fluorescent light. You might be surprised when he places the diamond upside down on the tray and has you look at the color through the pavilion (the backside of the diamond). This, however, is the most accurate way of seeing the fine nuances of color from one grade to another. Figure 5.1 shows you one common way of viewing diamonds for color.

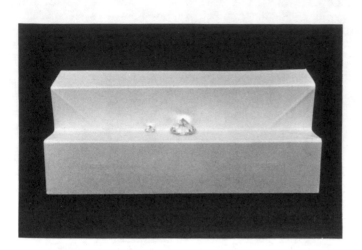

Fig. 5.1 A common way of viewing diamonds for color through the pavilion of the diamond. The small stone is a master stone weighing 0.30 carat. The larger stone is 4.30 carats.

When you are judging diamonds for color, remember the following tips:

♦ Judge diamond color against a non-reflective white background.

♦ Use comparison diamonds to determine a precise color grade. Even professional diamond graders realize that they cannot rely only on their color memory. They need master stones.

♦ Make sure the master stones and diamonds to be graded are clean. Dirt can affect the color grade.

♦ Place your diamond both to the right and to the left of the master stones. It's normal for it to look lighter on one side than the other.

♦ Pay attention to the grading environment. Color grading can be affected by the lighting, the color of the surroundings and your clothes, the air quality, and the country you live in (the sun's rays vary according to geographical regions), and the time of day and year.

♦ Be careful not to mistakenly downgrade larger diamonds. They often appear darker than small master stones of the same color grade because the color is easier to see.

♦ Remember that precise color grading can only be done with loose diamonds. The color of the metal surrounding diamonds set in jewelry influences the appearance of the diamonds. Consequently, their color can only be estimated.

Treated Diamonds & Fluorescent Diamonds

Suppose you could permanently transform a brownish tinted diamond into a more valuable looking green or orange diamond. Would you not be tempted to do so? Thanks to irradiation and heat treatments, permanent color changes in diamonds are possible. These treatments are accepted as legitimate trade practices and allow consumers to buy colored diamonds at more affordable prices.

Unfortunately, some people try to pass off their treated diamonds as naturally colored in order to get a higher price. So, before investing a high sum of money in a fancy colored diamond, consider having the stone tested by a reputable gem laboratory for possible color treatment. There's nothing wrong with color treatment as long as you are told about it and not charged natural color prices.

Not all diamond color treatments are permanent and legitimate. Many are temporary and done only with the intention of deceiving the buyer. Occasionally the girdle or back of the diamond is coated with a chemical or plastic to make it look less yellow. Sometimes bits of carbon paper under the prongs or a few dots of ink on the girdle are used to improve the color. In one instance a 9 1/2 carat fancy pink diamond at a major auction house was switched and replaced with a stone coated with pink nail polish.

If you deal with a reputable jeweler, you won't need to worry about such deceitful tricks. You should, however, be aware of them so you can avoid being taken by dishonest vendors that offer doctored up diamonds at prices which are too good to be true.

Occasionally people get concerned when they see their diamond glow under ultraviolet lights. They suspect that it has been artificially treated when it just has a natural fluorescence. The GIA estimates that about 50% of gem diamonds are fluorescent. Blue fluorescence, the most common type, can mask undesirable yellow tints of a diamond viewed under the sun's ultraviolet rays. This means fluorescence can be a positive feature provided it isn't so strong that it makes the diamond look cloudy.

When shopping for diamonds, you may hear the term *blue-white*. Originally it was meant to refer to colorless diamonds with blue fluorescence, but the term has been so misused that the Federal Trade Commission in the United States has prohibited its use.

How Objective are Color Grades?

Color grades are not as objective as people would like them to be. Even when the grader is someone as highly respected as the GIA, the color grade can be questioned. Russell Shor, senior editor of the *Jewelers' Circular Keystone* magazine, points out in their September

1987 issue that sometimes the grades of diamonds change when they are sent back to the GIA for re-examination. Most of the differences, however, involve borderline cases, and a change of more than one color grade is rare.

The fact that no gem trade lab in the world will guarantee their grades or accept liability for their grading errors is a good indication that color grading is subjective. Color measuring instruments exist, but normally grading has to be done by people because how they perceive the color is what's important. Some of the problems that make it so difficult for people to grade color objectively are:

♦ The size of master stones (color comparison diamonds) is usually much smaller than the stone being graded. Slight nuances of color are harder to detect in small stones than in large ones, so comparing stones of different sizes can be misleading.

♦ The proportions of master stones may be different than the stone being graded, creating differences in color perception.

♦ The shape and cutting style of master stones may be different from the diamond being graded. It is not easy to compare the color of a marquise or emerald-cut diamond to that of a round master stone.

♦ Sometimes flaws in a diamond can affect the way color is perceived during grading.

♦ A color grade represents a range of color not an exact color. Therefore a G color can be almost an F or almost an H, and a G- and an H+ can look about the same.

♦ Sometimes a diamond is color zoned meaning it has two grades of color. A choice or average has to be made between the two colors.

In spite of the complexity of grading diamonds, professionals still often agree on color grades. You should, however, expect buyers and sellers to have strong disagreements, particularly when the color lies between two grades. After all, thousands of dollars can be at stake. For example, the wholesale price difference between a five-carat, internally flawless I and J color round diamond is listed as $5500 per carat (as per the September 1991 Rapaport price guide). In other words, the difference of only one color grade that the average consumer can't see could mean a difference in wholesale cost of up to $27,500 for a five-carat diamond.

Does the lack of objectivity mean that color grades are worthless? Of course not. Thanks to the establishment of international color grading systems, it's easier now to do comparison shopping. You can discuss minute nuances of color and negotiate purchases with people thousands of miles away.

Gemological laboratories are aware of the limitations of diamond grading, so they normally have more than one person examine each diamond. You need to be aware, too, of the limitations. If a jeweler tells you a stone is a G color and a gem lab calls it an H color, you shouldn't assume that the jeweler is incompetent or dishonest. If, however, a jeweler calls an unmounted K color diamond a G color, you would probably be better off doing business with another jeweler. An awareness of the limitations can also help you realize that some jewelers' prices may appear to be higher than other jewelers' when, in fact, they might be lower due to stricter grading. This is one reason why many jewelers don't like to quote prices over the phone. If they are strict graders, they know that their prices will be unfairly compared to other stores that overgrade their stones.

When you get a diamond back from an appraiser or gem lab, keep in mind that color grading is subjective. The report or certificate is not necessarily the last word. It is at best an independent, expert opinion.

Chapter Five Quiz

Select the correct answer(s). **More than one answer may be possible** and therefore required.

1. Fancies are:

   a. Diamonds decorated with lace and sequins.
   b. Any shape diamond except round.
   c. Diamonds with a natural body color other than light yellow, light brown, or light gray.
   d. Diamonds that have been artificially colored by irradiation and heat treatments.

2. A jeweler shows you a blue stone and identifies it as a diamond. The price seems very low for a blue diamond.

   a. You should assume that the jeweler doesn't know the difference between a sapphire and a diamond.
   b. You should buy it at once since the jeweler probably doesn't realize that naturally blue diamonds are very expensive.
   c. You should suspect that the stone has been artificially colored if it's a diamond.

3. You ask a jeweler you don't know to tell you what color the diamond in your yellow gold ring is. He tells you it's impossible for him to give you a precise color grade on the spot. This probably means that the jeweler:

   a. Doesn't know how to color grade diamonds.
   b. Feels that doctors and other professionals don't give out free services so why should he.
   c. Doesn't want to admit that your diamond is a better color than anything he has in his store.
   d. Knows that your diamond should be examined out of its mounting with comparison stones for accurate color grading. Otherwise only an estimate grade can be given.

4. One of the jewelry stores in a local shopping mall is having a special diamond ring promotion. Lourdes is amazed at how much lower the prices are than the other stores in the same mall. She can assume that

   a. There is a good chance that light brown or yellow diamonds were used in the promotional rings.
   b. The more expensive jewelry stores are owned by a bunch of greedy crooks.
   c. The store with the lower prices will soon go out of business.

5. Which of the following can affect your perception of diamond color?

    a.   The color of your clothes.
    b.   The city you live in.
    c.   The ten martinis you had the night before.
    d.   The lighting.
    e.   All of the above.

6. Becky wants a 1.00 carat D or E color diamond, and her jeweler tells her that he does not have any diamonds of that color and size in stock.

    a.   She should assume that he only sells poor quality diamonds.
    b.   She should ask if he can get a diamond that color and size.
    c.   She should assume he has a very limited selection of diamonds

7. You're looking at a diamond ring and you note a distinct yellowish tint in the diamond. What is a possible color grade for the diamond?

    a.   E
    b.   H
    c.   I.
    d.   top silver

8. Champagne diamonds

    a.   Have an exotic, valuable color.
    b.   Have a brownish tint.
    c.   Cost less than "white" diamonds.
    d.   None of the above

Answers: 1. b and c,   2. c,   3. b and d,   4. a,   5. e,   6. b,   7. c and d   8. b and c.

6

Judging Clarity

Imagine looking into a colorless kaleidoscope and seeing amid the geometric patterns things resembling miniature galaxies, rainbows, abstract sculptures, feathers, fishing lines, eroded canyons, or diamond crystals. That's what it can be like to look at a diamond through a microscope.

Sometimes when you look, all you can see is a geometric pattern. The diamond might be playing hide and seek with you. It expects you to tilt it and turn it upside down or sideways and spotlight it in different ways. Then out of nowhere, you may see some specks, ripples, or indentations. The specks might be minute crystals. They might also be dust particles on the surface that got tired of floating in air.

When you try to find the forms within a stone and marks on its exterior, you are analyzing its clarity. **Clarity** is the degree to which a stone is free from external marks called **blemishes** and internal features called **inclusions**. Together they represent the **clarity characteristics** or **clarity features** of the stone. You may be more familiar with terms such as *flaws, imperfections,* or *defects.* Gemologists prefer not to use these terms because of their negative connotations. A replacement for the term *blemish* should be found, too, because not all blemishes detract from the appearance or value of a diamond, despite what the term implies.

It can be to your advantage to buy a diamond with inclusions and blemishes. They can be proof that it is authentic and natural. They can act as a fingerprint and help protect you from having your diamond switched. They can lower the price of the diamond without affecting its beauty. They can make you feel your diamond is special. So, if you're buying a diamond for personal enjoyment, you don't need to know how to find one that is flawless. You do need to know, however, what flaws will make your diamond less attractive and less durable.

Fig. 6.1 A very cloudy diamond

Fig. 6.2 A long deep crack

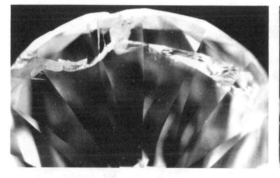

Fig. 6.3 A large threatening crack

Fig. 6.4 A badly chipped round diamond

Fig. 6.5 A chipped baguette

Fig. 6.6 A crack that looks like a big white blotch

Flaws to Avoid

If you are looking for an attractive, durable stone, you should avoid choosing a diamond with the following flaws:

♦ **Large, obvious milky or cloudy areas** (fig. 6.1). These diminish the transparency and brilliance considered so desireable in a diamond. If you want a milky, yet pretty stone, consider buying a moonstone. It's less expensive and displays a unique, billowy, light effect as it is moved.

♦ **Big deep cracks** (fig. 6.2 & 6.3). These are a threat to the durability of a diamond, especially when they are so big that you can see them extending across a diamond with your naked eye. Diamonds worn in rings get knocked about and can be further damaged when large cracks are present.

♦ **Big chips** (fig. 6.4 & 6.5). Besides looking bad, big chips are likely to grow bigger through normal wear.

♦ **Big white, black, or colored lines and blotches that can easily be seen with the naked eye** (fig. 6.6). They represent inclusions and blemishes which can decrease the brilliancy of the diamond, threaten its durability, and mar its overall beauty. Sometimes diamonds with visible blotches and lines are good in earrings where they don't receive close scrutiny and a lot of hard wear.

In order to spot the above flaws, you don't need a magnifier. All that is needed is good eyesight. But if you're interested in accurately comparing diamond prices, you should learn to examine diamonds with a ten-power magnifier. You will then have a better understanding of the clarity categories that are so important for diamond pricing.

Examining Diamonds for Clarity

To examine a stone for clarity you need a ten-power magnifier, a lint free cloth, and a light source that allows light to be directed through the sides of the stone. An ordinary fluorescent desk lamp with a daylight type bulb will do. Tweezers or a stoneholder is also helpful. Jewelers often use a hand magnifier called a loupe (fig. 6.7). For those interested in owning a loupe, the business section of the phone book has stores listed under *Jewelers' Supplies & Findings*.

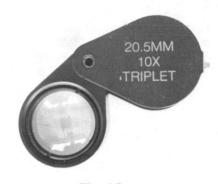

Fig. 6.7.

First verify that they have a fully corrected, ten-power, triplet loupe. The loupe salesman or a jeweler can show you some ways of holding and using it and help you select the model that is the most comfortable and clear.

There are a couple of guidelines you should remember about using a ten-power loupe. Hold the loupe 1/2 to 1 inch (13-25 mm.) away from the stone to bring it into focus. If you're examining a large stone, hold the loupe close to one eye (about 1 or 2 inches or 25-50 mm. from the eye) keeping both eyes open. The closer the loupe is to your eye, the greater your field of vision is.

If you're examining a lot of small stones less than 1/10 of a carat, try holding the loupe further away from your face and use both eyes to look at them. This will help prevent eyestrain.

The use of the loupe is not limited to the grading of gemstones. It can also be used to judge the quality of fabrics or the resolution of your computer printer. It can even help you determine if the black specks in your food are bugs or coarse pepper. Once you own a loupe you will find lots of uses for it.

When you have the necessary equipment, you can proceed as follows:

1. Clean the diamond. Usually rubbing it with a lint-free cloth is sufficient. Sometimes, though, you'll need to soak it in soap and water or ethyl alcohol or even have it professionally cleaned. Avoid touching the stone with your fingers as fingers can leave smudges.

2. Examine the stone from all angles with your naked eye. One of the criteria for assigning clarity grades is the visibility of the inclusions without magnification. Looking at the stone first with a loupe can mislead you into believing inclusions are eye visible when they aren't, because your mind has a tendency to see what it expects to see.

3. Examine the stone with a loupe from all angles. For viewing inclusions, the light should pass through the side of the stone; and for viewing surface blemishes, it should reflect off the stone. Using a microscope instead of a loupe should pose no problems. Most beginners even find it is easier to use.

Clarity Features

As you examine diamonds under magnification, you'll probably wonder what you are looking at. Listed below are some of the clarity features you'll see. Keep in mind that mother nature rarely repeats herself; you may find variations and combinations of these typical features.

Internal features (Inclusions):

♦ **Cracks** of various sizes are commonly seen in diamonds (fig. 6.8). If the cracks are small, normally you need not worry about them. The crack in figure 6.8 does not weaken the diamond and is not visible from a face-up position, so this stone still received a very high grade of VS$_2$ (very slightly included) from the GIA. You should however be concerned about big cracks like the one in figure 6.2. When cracks are jagged, they're called **fractures**. When they're straight and flat, they're called **cleavages**. Both types of cracks are often called **feathers** due to the close resemblance.

♦ **Crystals** of all sorts of interesting shapes and sizes are also common in diamonds (figs. 6.9 - 6.12). Over 24 different minerals have been identified as crystal inclusions in diamond, but the most frequent type crystal seen is another diamond. Crystals can lower the clarity grade of your diamond, but they can also turn it into a collector's item.

♦ **Black, white, and colored spots** are usually just crystals and cracks (fig. 6.13). If they look like tiny dots, they are called **pinpoints**. Sometimes you may hear black spots referred to as *carbon spots*, but this can mislead people into believing that coal particles are in their diamonds. Eric Bruton discusses this on page 385 of his book *Diamonds* and says, "Dark inclusions in diamond were for generations called *carbon spots*, although it is now known that amorphous carbon does not occur as inclusions." More often than not, spots that look black are actually transparent.

♦ **Clouds** are hazy or milky areas in a diamond that occasionally resemble a galaxy (fig. 6.14). Most clouds are made up of crystals too tiny to see individually under ten-power magnification. Clouds may be hard to find in diamonds with high clarity grades. When clouds are large and dense, they can make your diamond look undesirably white.

♦ **Growth or grain lines** are fine lines or ripples caused by irregular crystallization (fig. 6.15). Sometimes diamonds look hazy when many of these lines are present.

♦ **Cavities** are large indentations where chunks of the diamond are missing (fig. 6.16). They may look like mountain ranges or eroded canyons.

♦ **Laser drill holes look** like suspended fishing lines (fig. 6.17). They're actually tiny holes drilled into the diamond with a laser beam, allowing black spots to be bleached out with chemicals. This treatment is considered legitimate and normally improves the appearance. There are times, however, when the diamond looks worse after drilling due to the resulting long white drill holes. To see laser holes you usually have to tilt the diamond or view it from the side.

External features (surface blemishes):

♦ **Scratches, nicks, pits, and abraded facet edges** are not considered as serious as inclusions because they can often be polished away.

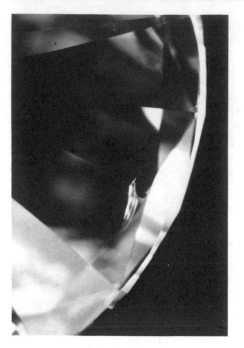

Fig. 6.8 A minor crack

Fig. 6.9 A crystal inclusion

Fig. 6.10 A diamond crystal in a 5 carat diamond

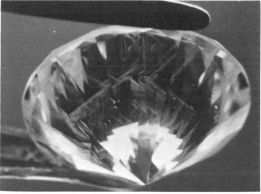

Fig. 6.11 Side view of the 5 carat diamond in figure 6.10

Fig. 6.12 An olivine crystal in a diamond

Fig. 6.13 Black spots that are crystals and reflections of crystals

Fig. 6.14 A cloud near the culet of a diamond

Fig. 6.15 Grain lines

Fig. 6.16 Large cavity on the pavilion of a diamond

Fig. 6.17 Laser drill holes

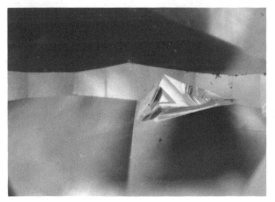

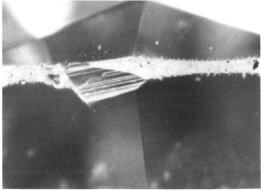

Fig. 6.18 A natural with trigons

Fig. 6.19 A natural with step-like ridges

♦ **Extra facets** are additions to the normal number of facets (flat, geometric diamond surfaces). They are usually added to polish away a flaw or save diamond weight. They don't affect the clarity grade of a diamond if they are on the pavilion and can't be seen face up at ten-power magnification.

♦ **Naturals** are part of the original surface of the diamond crystal left unpolished (fig. 6.18 & 6.19). Sometimes they have step-like ridges or triangular forms (called **trigons**) on them that indicate your stone is truly a diamond. Naturals do not affect the clarity grade if they are confined to the girdle and do not distort the girdle outline.

Clarity Grading Explained

Now that we have identified diamond inclusions and blemishes, we are ready to look at how they affect clarity grades. There are various grading systems, but those that are best known resemble the one developed by the GIA (Gemological Institute of America). You can make yourself understood to any knowledgeable diamond dealer or jeweler in the world using the GIA system.

Clarity grade descriptions of all the major systems assume a trained grader working with ten-power fully corrected magnification and effective illumination. The GIA defines their clarity grades under these conditions as follows:

GIA Clarity Grades*	
* For trained graders using 10-power magnification & proper lighting.	
Fl	**Flawless**, no blemishes or inclusions.
IF	**Internally flawless**, no inclusions and only insignificant blemishes.
VVS_1 & VVS_2	**Very, very slightly included**, minute inclusions that are difficult to see.
VS_1 & VS_2	**Very slightly included**, minor inclusions ranging from difficult to somewhat easy to see.
SI_1 & SI_2	**Slightly included**, noticeable inclusions that are easy (SI_1) or very easy (SI_2) to see.
I_1, I_2, & I_3	**Imperfect**, obvious inclusions that usually are eye-visible face up; in I_3, distinctions are based on the combined effect on durability, transparency, and brilliance.

These definitions may seem unscientific, and in fact they are unscientific. However, trained and experienced graders nearly always agree on the clarity grade; an untrained or inexperienced grader will have difficulty in determining clarity grades consistently. Diamonds were not created to fit into well-defined categories. Categories had to be created to differentiate already existing diamonds. This was not an easy process.

The first diamond grading system was introduced by the GIA in the late 1920's. Since then it has been debated and modified. The present system allows people throughout the world to compare and visualize degrees of clarity that are imperceptible to the naked eye.

Diamond grading is an art. That means it requires practice, and a good way of getting this practice is to start examining diamonds with the help of your jeweler. But before you look at diamonds, try forming a general mental picture of some of the clarity grades by studying the examples in figures 6.20 to 6.25. There are no examples of the grades from Flawless to VS_1, because the differences don't show up well in photographs. Expect actual diamonds to look different than these photos due to the two-dimensional nature of printing and the focusing problems of microscope photography. Further details of all the categories are given below.

Flawless (Fl)	Flawless diamonds are rarely used in jewelry. Ordinary wear could cause them to lose their flawless status.
Internally Flawless (IF)	Diamonds with no inclusions and only insignificant blemishes, such as tiny pits and scratches that are easily removed with repolishing, can be classified internally flawless. It is unlikely that your jeweler has IF or Fl diamonds in stock. He might, however, be able to locate one for you.
VVS_1 & VVS_2	These diamonds have inclusions so small that the average person would not be able to find them under ten-power magnification. Even trained diamond graders may have to view the stone from several positions to find the inclusion. Jewelers seldom keep these stones in stock, especially if they are one carat or more.
VS_1	A layperson would have a very hard time finding the very small crystals, clouds, feathers, or pinpoints that characterize this grade. Sometimes, he may never find them under ten-power magnification. Some stores keep large VS_1 diamonds in stock, but if they have a wide selection of them, be suspicious of overgrading because they are not readily available in large quantities.
VS_2	Diamonds with this classification have the same types of inclusions as VS_1 stones but the inclusions are either more numerous, larger, or easier to see (fig. 6.20).

SI$_1$ Even though this is the seventh clarity grade from the top, this is still an excellent stone. If you look at it with the unaided eye, you probably can't see any inclusions. If you look at it with ten-times magnification, you might notice small feathers, clouds, or crystals (fig. 6.21).

SI$_2$ Sometimes you can see the inclusions of these stones through the pavilion (bottom) of the stone with the naked eye, but normally, the inclusions are not visible through the crown (fig 6.22). An exception to this would be with large diamonds and with emerald-cut diamonds. As the GIA points out, inclusions in such diamonds are easier to see because of their larger facets. The inclusions of the SI grades generally do not affect the durability of the stone.

I$_1$ The inclusions of this grade are obvious at ten-power magnification, but in small brilliant-cut diamonds, they are barely visible to the unaided eye through the crown (fig. 6.23). This can be a good clarity grade choice for people on a limited budget who want a nice diamond. Often a well-cut I$_1$ looks better than a poorly cut SI diamond.

I$_2$ The inclusions are easily visible to the unaided eye and may affect the beauty and durability of the diamond (fig. 6.24). This grade is frequently used in discount jewelry.

I$_3$ These diamonds often look shattered, as if they'd been hammered. Sometimes they have no cracks, but they're so filled with crystal inclusions that they have a muddy gray or whitish look (fig. 6.25). An I$_3$ grade would be unacceptable to someone interested in a brilliant and transparent diamond.

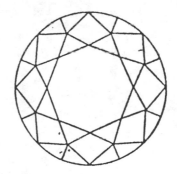

Fig. 6.20 VS$_2$

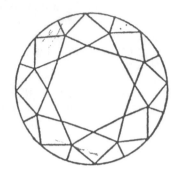

Fig. 6.21   SI$_1$

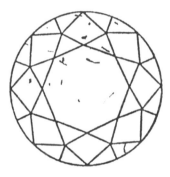

Fig. 6.22   SI$_2$

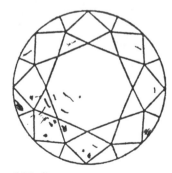

Fig. 6.23   I$_1$

Fig. 6.24 I_2

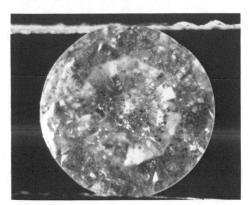

Fig. 6.25 I_3

Clarity grading requires more than identification of diamond inclusions. An overall visual impression must be formed of the diamond with and without ten-power magnification, and the grading conditions must be considered. Keep in mind the following:

♦ Only approximate clarity grades can be assigned to diamonds set in jewelry. Metal prongs can hide inclusions and blemishes.

♦ Diamonds must be clean for accurate grading.

♦ Big inclusions generally lower grades more than small inclusions. Usually one or two of the largest inclusions establish the clarity grade.

♦ The type of inclusion can have a dramatic effect on the grade. For example, a small feather (crack) will tend to lower a grade more than a pinpoint inclusion.

♦ Dark inclusions tend to lower grades more than colorless and white inclusions. Sometimes, however, white inclusions stand out more than black ones due to their position.

♦ Inclusions under the table (in the center) of the diamond tend to lower grades more than those near the girdle (around the edges).

♦ If it's easy for you to see inclusions through the top of a diamond without maginification, it's fairly certain that the stone is an I grade.

♦ Your overall impression of a diamond's clarity can be affected by the diamonds it is compared to. A diamond will look better when viewed with low clarity diamonds than with high clarity ones.

♦ The clarity grade of a given stone is not fixed. It can change due to daily wear on the diamond. For example, if a flawless stone is scratched, the highest grade it can be assigned without repolishing is IF.

♦ The clarity grades can also change depending on who the grader is. A one grade difference between two experienced graders is not uncommon.

♦ Diamonds of the same clarity grade are not always equally desirable. In fact, an I_1 stone can look better than an SI_2 stone when set. That's why it's important to look at a diamond under magnification instead of just relying on a clarity grade to choose a diamond.

♦ Diamonds are normal if they have inclusions, not defective.

How Clarity Affects Price

As you might expect, **the higher the clarity grade of a diamond, the more it costs.** Also, usually the higher the color grade of a diamond, the more the clarity grade affects its cost. For example, in January 1993, the Rapaport wholesale diamond price guide listed a one-carat, round, D-color, IF diamond as about 10 times higher than a D-color, I_3 diamond of the same size, whereas a one-carat, K-color IF was priced about 4 times higher than a K-color I_3.

There is no systematic increase in cost as the clarity grade gets higher. For example, on the Rapaport price guide, a two-carat, round, G-color VS_2 was $1100 more per carat than an H-color VS_2. A two-carat, G-color VS_1 was $500 more per carat than an H-color VS_1. Diamond pricing is based more on supply and demand than it is on rational systems.

When buying diamonds, it's important to realize that clarity differences that go unnoticed by laypeople looking through a microscope can mean thousands of dollars in value. For example, a 5-carat, D-color, IF diamond can have a wholesale value of $100,000 more than a 5-carat, D-color, VVS_2 diamond. Therefore, if you are planning on investing in a high clarity grade diamond, it is well worth your money to pay for an independent lab grading report on it before purchasing or insuring it. Grading reports can be expensive so they are seldom done on low-clarity diamonds. Even when a grading report comes with the stone, you will probably have paid for the report indirectly, as reflected in the cost of the stone.

Dealing with a reputable jeweler will also help insure getting the quality you pay for. Grading differences and questions can arise with any jeweler or lab, but with someone reputable, you have the peace of mind of knowing that you could get a refund if there were any problems with the grading.

Chapter Six Quiz

Select the correct answer.

1. When used for clarity grading, *VS* means :

   a. Vague scratches
   b. Various spots
   c. Very slightly included
   d. Very substandard

2. You're in a jewelry store and the owner asks to see your diamond ring. He places it under a microscope and tells you the diamond has a small crack in the center so it is a lousy diamond. When you look through the microscope, you are able to see a very small, fine line in the diamond. This means:

   a. Your diamond is defective.
   b. The diamond will soon crack into pieces.
   c. The owner is unprofessional, and he is giving you misleading information.
   d. The owner is a true diamond expert and deserves your patronage.

3. You want to sell an old diamond ring. The total weight of the diamonds is four carats. You ask a jeweler how much she will pay you for it, but she says she can't give you a price until the ring is cleaned. This means:

   a. The jeweler does not want to buy the ring.
   b. The jeweler wants to embarrass you.
   c. Your ring is so valuable that the jeweler can't afford to buy it; and even if she could, her clientele probably wouldn't be able to afford it. .
   d. The jeweler knows that the color and clarity of diamonds cannot be accurately determined unless the stones are clean; and without this information, it's not possible to determine the value.

4. Your boyfriend gives you a diamond for your birthday. When you look at it with a loupe, you can easily see some black spots in the center of the diamond. You can't see them or any other blemishes or inclusions with your naked eye. This means:

   a. Your diamond is worthless and your boyfriend is cheap.
   b. It's possible that your diamond has a clarity grade of SI_2.
   c. It's possible that your diamond has a clarity grade of VVS_2.
   d. Your diamond is tainted with coal particles.

5. Which of the following clarity features is **least** likely to affect the clarity grade of a diamond.

    a. naturals
    b. clouds
    c. feathers
    d. crystals

6. You're looking at a diamond, and you can see white spots in it with your naked eye. What is a possible clarity grade for the diamond?

    a. VVS_1
    b. VS_2
    c. IF
    d. I_2

7. You have a friend that claims to be a gemologist. When you ask him to estimate the clarity grade of the diamond in a solitaire ring you just bought, he hesitates and says that it looks like it's at least an SI. You should assume that:

    a. Your friend is either an incompetent gemologist or not one at all since he can't give you a clear-cut answer.
    b. Your friend is embarrassed to tell you the true clarity grade of the diamond because he doesn't want to hurt your feelings or imply that your jeweler sold you a poor diamond.
    c. Your friend's eyesight is probably failing.
    d. Your friend knows it's difficult to assign clarity grades to diamonds set in rings because the settings can hide clarity characteristics, especially when the clarity grades are potentially high.

8. Which of the following statements is **false**?

    a. A difference of one or two clarity grades can sometimes affect the value of a diamond by thousands of dollars.
    b. It is normal for diamonds to have blemishes and inclusions.
    c. There are no advantages to buying a diamond with inclusions and blemishes.
    d. It's possible for an I_1 diamond that's mounted in a ring to look better than an SI_2 diamond.

Answers: 1. c,   2. c,   3. d,   4. b,   5. a,   6. d,   7. d,   8. c.

7

Judging Cut

If it is not cut right, a flawless D color diamond might be considered a reject by a diamond dealer. A poor cut can make a diamond look dull, glassy, bulky, and too small for its weight. A good cut can increase its brilliance, sparkle, durability, and aesthetic appeal.

The term *cut* is sometimes confusing because it has a variety of meanings. Jewelers use it to refer to:

♦ The **shape** of a gemstone (e.g. round or oval)

♦ The **cutting style** (e.g. brilliant or step cut, single or full cut)

♦ The **proportions** of a stone (e.g. big or small table facet, deep or shallow pavilion)

♦ The **finish** of a stone (e.g. polishing marks or smooth flawless surface, misshapen or symmetrical facets)

The proportions and finish are also called the **make** of the stone and will be the focus of this chapter. Shape and cutting style were discussed in chapter three.

What is a Poorly Cut Diamond?

Gem experts can agree on what colors and clarity of diamonds will command the highest prices, but if you were to ask them what the most ideal and valuable way to cut a diamond was, you would get a variety of answers. However, you could get them to agree that a diamond is poorly cut if the following characteristics can be noted with the naked eye:

Fig. 7.1 A fish-eye, shallow-pavilion diamond

Fig. 7.2 A dark center, deep-pavilion diamond with a very large table

Fig. 7.3 a A dark bow-tie that appears to cut the stone in two

Fig. 7.3 b A well-cut marquise without a bow-tie.

Fig. 7.4 An extremely thick girdle

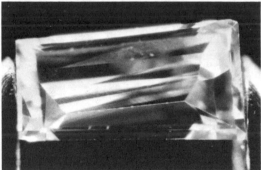

Fig. 7.5 A tapered baguettte with unsymmetrical and misshapen facets

♦ A **white circle** resembling a skinny donut in the face-up view of a diamond (fig. 7.1). In the trade, this is called a **fish-eye** diamond, and it is the result of the reflection of the girdle when the pavilion (the bottom cone-shaped portion of the diamond) is too shallow. The thicker and more prominent the white circle the poorer the cut is. Besides looking bad, fish-eye diamonds usually lack the brilliance of well-cut diamonds.

♦ An obvious black circular area in the center of the diamond when viewed face up (fig. 7.2). **Very dark centers,** also called **nailheads,** indicate that the diamond's pavilion was cut too deep. Their presence interrupts the mass of white light that diamonds are supposed to radiate back to you.

♦ **Large, obvious, dark, bow-tie** shaped areas in fancies such as marquise or oval diamonds (figs. 7.3). Most fancy-shaped diamonds have at least a slight bow-tie, but when it is so pronounced that it is distracting, the bow-tie becomes an undesirable feature. Bow-ties result when the pavilion facets are not angled properly or when the pavilion is cut too deep.

♦ An **extremely thick girdle** (the rim around the diamond separating the crown from the pavilion) (fig. 7.4). Not only do very thick girdles decrease the brilliance of your stone, they also make your stone appear small for its weight because so much diamond mass is concentrated at the girdle area instead of spread out across the stone.

♦ An **obviously unsymmetrical shape** (fig. 7.5). No diamond is 100% symmetrical, but when the diamond looks lopsided or the major facets are strikingly irregular, the lack of symmetry is unacceptable.

Judging Diamond Profiles

When you buy a diamond, be sure to look at its profile with and without magnification. The side view will show you:

♦ If the crown is too thick or too thin.

♦ If the pavilion is too deep or too shallow.

♦ If the girdle is too thick or too thin.

♦ If the diamond is too lumpy or too flat.

Figure 7.6 reviews some diamond terminology and serves as an example of a well-proportioned round brilliant.

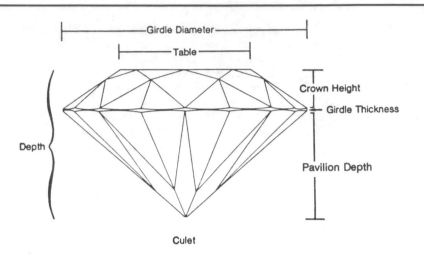

Girdle Diameter

Table

Crown Height

Girdle Thickness

Depth

Pavilion Depth

Culet

Fig. 7.6

Measure the depth and girdle diameter of the diagrammed diamond and then divide the depth by the girdle diameter. The depth should be about 60% of the diameter, a good ratio for a round diamond. When judging a fancy-shape diamond, divide the depth by the width. The GIA suggests that the depth is normally in the range of 55 to 65% of the width of the diamond.

Next, estimate how many times thicker or higher the crown is than the pavilion. In figure 7.6, the pavilion is a little more than 2 1/2 times as deep as the crown. The GIA states that most well-made diamonds have pavilions about 2 1/2 to 3 1/2 times as thick as their crowns.

Judging diamond proportions with ratios and measurements can be tedious and time consuming. By just studying examples of good and bad profiles, you can learn to make quick visual judgments. Look at figures 7.7 to 7.11 below:

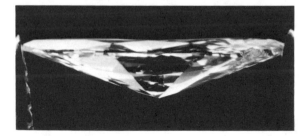

Figure 7.7 is an example of a marquise diamond with too thin of a crown and too flat of a profile. Face up, the stone looks big for its weight. Since the crown doesn't rise much, it can't form a prism to emit flashes of rainbow colors called fire. This diamond lacks the sparkle of a well-cut diamond and is fragile at the thin, pointed ends.

Figure 7.8 is an example of a chunky marquise diamond with too thick of a girdle and a bulging pavilion. Face up this stone will look small for its weight. The buyer will pay for extra weight that diminishes the brilliance and helps create a black bow-tie.

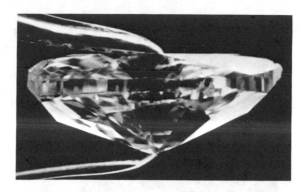

The round brilliant in figure 7.9 is another example of a diamond with too thin of a crown. It also has too deep of a pavilion. This adds to the weight and detracts from the appearance face up.

Figure 7.10 is an example of a well-cut diamond. Note the relationship of the crown height to the pavilion depth, about 3 to 1. This means that the pavilion depth can be about 43% of the girdle diameter. This prevents the diamond from having a fish-eye or dark center. The proper height and angles of the crown lets the diamond display a good balance of brilliance and fire. Even though the crown is slightly unsymmetrical, it does not detract from the overall appearance. It's hard to find a diamond with perfect symmetry.

High-crown diamonds like the one in figure 7.11 look small for their weight when set. They also have an odd appearance when viewed face up (fig. 7.12). Their upper girdle and bezel facets look crinkly. The crown of the diamond in 7.12 is so high that it's hard to bring it in focus through a microscope, but you can still get an idea of what it would look like through a loupe. Compare the diamond in figure 7.12 with the diamonds in figures 6.20 to 6.22 of Chapter Six, which have an acceptable crown height.

Fig. 7.11. High crown

Fig. 7.12. Face-up view of diamond with high crown.

Judging the Table

When judging the table (the big, top, center facet forming an octagon on a round stone), you should ask three main questions:

♦ Is the table too big (fig. 7.2) or too small (fig. 7.13)?

♦ Is the table well-centered?

♦ Does the table have a symmetrical shape such as a regular octagon or rectangle.

Fig. 7.13. Small Table

76

There is a difference of opinion as to what is the best table size for a diamond. Diamond cutters in Europe have tended to prefer bigger tables than American diamond cutters. Some Americans feel that the ideal table width is 53% of the girdle diameter. Some Europeans would slightly downgrade a 53% table. Perhaps most diamond experts would agree that the table width should be more than 51% and less than 68% of the girdle diameter. (Figure 7.13 has about a 50% table and figure 7.2 has about a 74% table).

Why is table size important? If the table is too big, the diamond will not have much sparkle and fire. If the table is too small, the diamond will not display enough brilliance, and it will probably look small for its weight. Diamonds with big tables often have thin crowns, and those with small tables tend to have have high crowns.

How do you determine table size? It's possible to divide the maximum table width by the average girdle diameter or width to get a percentage. However, if you note the table size of the diamonds you look at, you will start making quick mental judgments as to whether the table is too big, too small, or acceptable. You don't need to calculate an exact table percentage. If the brilliance and sparkle of the diamond is impressive, then the table size is probably acceptable.

Judging the Girdle

A well-cut girdle will not be:

♦ Too thick or too thin

♦ Very uneven in thickness (fig 7.14)

♦ Wavy or slanted (fig 7.15)

♦ Rough or bearded (fig 7.16)

Diamonds with thin girdles are hard to set and easy to chip. Diamonds with thick girdles have reduced brilliance, look smaller than they weigh, and are also hard to set. The judgment of girdle thickness is best done with the eye, with and without magnification. If the girdle looks like a wide band encircling the diamond, it is probably too thick. If the girdle is sharp and you can hardly see it, then it is probably too thin. Figures 7.14 to 7.19 show girdles of acceptable and unacceptable thickness as well as girdles that are wavy and uneven.

Fig. 7.14 A very thick and uneven girdle

Fig. 7.15 A very thin, wavy girdle

Fig. 7.16 A bearded girdle

Fig. 7.17 An extremely thick, faceted girdle

Fig. 7.18 An acceptable bruted girdle

Fig. 7.19 An acceptable bruted girdle

As you examine diamond girdles you will notice three types:

♦ **Faceted** (fig. 7.17)

♦ **Bruted**, with a frosty or waxy look (figs. 7.18 & 7.19)

♦ **Polished** with no facets, looking like a clear continuous rim of glass going around the diamond (too clear to show up well in a photo)

Bruted girdles should be smooth and precision cut. If they are rough like sandpaper they can trap dirt, giving the girdle a gray, dark look. Sometimes, girdles have fringes looking like whiskers and hairs (fig. 7.16). They are appropriately called **bearded girdles** and can lower the clarity grade of diamonds--especially those of high clarity.

Judging Brilliance

Sometimes we get so involved in analyzing the color, clarity, and cut of a diamond that we forget to notice if the diamond is brilliant or not. A diamond can be well cut, yet not brilliant. The chemical composition of the diamond, its color, its shape, its cutting style, dirt, and inclusions also affect the brilliance. If, however, a diamond is highly brilliant, one can assume it is well-proportioned.

Learning to recognize degrees of diamond brilliance is a challenge and can best be done by comparing diamonds and other gemstones of varying brilliance. The stones should first be cleaned and then viewed face up and face down. When dull and glassy stones are viewed next to brilliant stones, the differences become obvious. It's hard to explain brilliance with words, but it can be described as a mirror-like quality resulting from the reflection of light off the surface and interior of a stone. The greater the light return the greater the brilliance. Diamonds have the potential of displaying a brilliance unmatched by any other gemstone. This is due to their optical properties and to their superior hardness which allows them to have an unusually high polish.

Before buying a diamond, take a moment to simply ask yourself if it looks brilliant, both with the naked eye and under magnification. When you pay diamond prices, you want to get diamond brilliance.

How the Quality of the Cut Affects Price

Wholesale price guides take into consideration shape, weight, color, and clarity, but they neglect to indicate exactly how the make (proportions and finish) of a diamond affects its price. This is because no agreed upon price categories have been established for the quality of the cut. Yet it plays a large role in determining the value of a diamond. Poor-make diamonds can be discounted as much as 50%, but this discounting is done in a very subjective manner.

Diamond dealers often buy mixed lots (assortments) of diamonds from suppliers in Belgium, Israel, and India. After buying them, the dealer has to sort them with a loupe into categories ranging from the highest to the lowest qualities. During this process, his main considerations are cut, clarity, and brilliance because the lots usually have already been sorted for general size and color.

Suppose a dealer picks up a VVS (near flawless), flat-pavilion, fish-eye stone. He might place it in the same category as a well-cut I_1 or I_2 (imperfect) stone and assign it the same per-carat price. A VVS stone with an extremely thick girdle and high crown (heavy make) might be priced like a well-cut SI_2 or I_1 stone.

Dealers and diamond jewelry manufacturers can also buy presorted, cheap lots of poor-make diamonds. But no matter how the diamonds are sold, experienced diamond buyers expect to pay less for poorly cut stones. Fish-eyes, heavy makes, and dull, lifeless diamonds are particularly noted for their lower values. Small deviations in symmetry and rough or uneven girdles do not change the value much because they can be corrected with little loss of diamond weight.

The lack of formal guidelines for pricing poor-make diamonds may be dismaying, but it need not be. Why should anyone want to invest so much money in a diamond whose beauty is diminished by major cutting defects? Man has control over a stone's cut, so well-cut diamonds will always be available as long as there is a demand for such quality. Perfectly cut diamonds, however, will never be available. Minute cutting defects will always be present. The trick is to learn to distinguish the minor from the major cutting defects. You can learn to do this by paying attention to the cut as you shop for diamonds. By looking at some well-cut diamonds, you will then have a model by which to judge other diamonds. If you can recognize a fine-cut, brilliant diamond, you are well on your way to spotting value.

Chapter Seven Quiz

True or False?

1. Diamonds of the same shape, color, clarity, and carat weight always have the same value.

2. Diamonds with thin crowns and big tables generally have less sparkle and fire (flashes of rainbow colors) than those with higher crowns and smaller tables.

3. The term *cut* has a variety of meanings that apply to diamonds.

4. The brilliance of a diamond is determined only by its cut.

5. Extremely thick girdles can make diamonds appear small for their weight.

6. It's easy to find diamonds with perfect symmetry.

7. The diamond trade has no formal guidelines for determining exactly how the quality of the cut affects the price of a diamond.

8. Dark bow-ties increase the value of fancy-shaped diamonds.

9. The quality of the cut can play a large role in determining the value of a diamond.

10. A well-cut diamond can lack brilliance.

11. If a lab document says the polish and finish of a diamond is good, this means the diamond is well-proportioned.

12. A good way to shop for diamonds is to ask for example, "How much is a 1-carat, G-color, VS_2 diamond?"

Answers:

1. F   The proportions and brilliance of a diamond also affect its value.

2. T

3. T

4. F   A diamond's clarity, color, and chemical composition also affect its brilliance.

5. T

6. F

7. T

8. F

9. T

10. T   A diamond's clarity, color, and chemical composition also affect its brilliance.

11. F   Finish refers to the quality of just the surface of the stone. Even if the finish is good, the diamond may be poorly proportioned and lackluster.

12. F.   A question such as this would indicate that you are more interested in grades than diamond beauty. Salespeople might then take advantage of you by either misrepresenting the grades of their diamonds or by selling you a poorly cut stone that might be worth 30 to 40% less than a well-cut one.

Instead of asking the price of a specific color and clarity grade, give salespeople an idea of the size, color and clarity range you are interested in and tell them you'd like a well-cut stone. Then when they show you the diamond(s), ask why they feel it's well-cut. Salespeople who are knowledgeable will be able to give specific reasons. They may even have you compare it to one which is poorly cut so you can see the difference.

8

Diamond or Imitation?

Anyone can be fooled by imitations, even diamond experts. However, by doing the following tests, you can reduce your chances of being fooled.

See-through Test
Look at the stone face up. Can you see through it? If you can, it's probably an imitation (In some cases a poor cut or the presence of dirt or grease makes it possible to see through a diamond). The see-through test can also be done by placing a clean, round stone face down on newsprint (fig 8.1). If you can see the letters through the stone, it probably is an imitation. For fancy shapes such as ovals and pears, it's best to limit this test to the face-up view because often, you can see through their pavilions.

If you plan to examine stones in antique jewelry, you should be aware that the diamonds may have a see-through effect due to the different cut and the large culet.

Tilt Test
Tilt the stone against a dark background. Can you see an obvious, dark, fan-shaped area (fig. 8.2)? If you can, it's doubtful that it is a diamond. This test is a variation of the see-through test, but it's easier to do on mounted stones. It also works best on round diamonds.

Fig. 8.1 See-through test. Note how the print cannot be seen through the diamond in the lower center. To the top left, is a synthetic spinel and to the top right, is a cubic zirconia.

Fig. 8.2 Tilt test. Note the black fan-shaped area of the synthetic spinel to the right of the diamond.

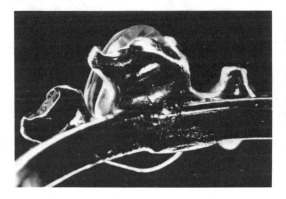

Fig. 8.3 Glass stones in closed-back settings

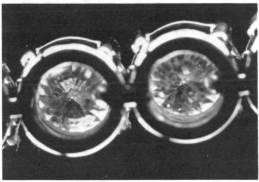

Fig. 8.4 Diamonds in open-back settings

Rainbow Colors Test

Move the stone under a light and note how strong the flashes of rainbow colors are in comparison to a diamond under the same light. If the rainbow colors (also called **dispersion** or **fire**) are a lot more obvious than your diamond, the stone may be synthetic rutile or strontium titanate. If they're less obvious, the stone may be an imitation or a diamond with a large table and a thin crown. This test is most useful for distinguishing diamond from synthetic rutile and strontium titanate, the two imitations which, like diamond, can be cut to have no see-through effect.

CZ (cubic zirconia) also displays more rainbow colors than diamond, but sometimes it's hard for the untrained eye to see the difference. It's particularly important to compare CZ and diamond under the same light. The rainbow colors are easier to see in sunlight and under incandescent light (from light bulbs) than under fluorescent light.

Closed-back Test

If the stone is set in jewelry, look at the back of the setting. Is the pavilion (bottom) of the stone blocked from view or enclosed in metal (fig. 8.3)? Normally, the bottom of a diamond is at least partially visible (fig. 8.4). Therefore, if you can only see the crown or top of the stone, you need to investigate carefully.

An open-back setting does not indicate that a stone is a diamond. Imitation diamonds are often set with the pavilion showing. But a completely closed back is often a sign that something is being hidden. Maybe the stone is a rhinestone (glass with a foil back). Maybe the stone is a diamond with a coating to improve its color. Maybe the stone is a single-cut diamond made to appear like a more expensive brilliant-cut diamond. No matter what might be hidden, to avoid being duped, it is best to buy a diamond in a setting with part of the pavilion showing if you're not dealing with someone you know and trust.

If you have antique jewelry, you should not assume that foil-backed stones in enclosed settings are rhinestones. Prior to the eighteenth century, it was common practice to put a foil backing on diamonds to improve their brilliance.

Recently, some jewelry manufacturers have used solid backs under channel-set diamonds to increase the rigidity of the channel mountings. This allows the diamonds to be set more securely. In most cases, however, it is still customary to set diamonds with part of the pavilion showing.

Price Test

Is the stone being sold at an unbelievably low price? If it is, it might be an imitation or stolen or defective merchandise. Jewelers have to pay a lot for diamonds, and they cannot stay in business if they sell their diamonds below their cost.

Thermal Conduction Test

GIA GEM Pocket Diamond Tester with warning buzzer

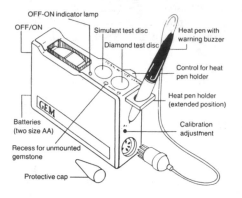

An easy, quick, and accurate way of determining if a stone is a diamond is to test it with an instrument like the GIA GEM pocket diamond tester (fig 8.5) which measures the heat conductivity of the stone. This test is based on the principle that diamonds conduct heat better than any stone used to imitate it. A metal probe or heat pen is pressed on a facet of the stone. Then the needle of the instrument's meter reads *diamond* or *imitation*. A thermal conductivity tester might be a worthwhile investment for people who are interested in buying diamond jewelry on a regular basis at auctions, flea markets, and from private individuals. The pocket tester in figure 8.5 can be purchased from the GIA Gem Instruments Corporation in New York City or in Santa Monica, California.

Fig. 8.5. (Courtesy of the GIA)

There are other tests for distinguishing diamonds from imitations, but many of them require special training or equipment. Nevertheless, you may be curious about how gemologists identify diamonds. Therefore, other methods have been listed below.

♦ The interior and exterior of the stone are examined under magnification. Certain features characterize diamonds such as naturals, trigons, laser drill holes, and included diamond crystals, which were discussed in chapter six. Imitations are often flawless or have gas bubbles.

♦ The stone is examined for transparency. Diamonds are noted for their high transparency, so if it looks hazy, it might be an imitation like cubic zirconia. There are, however, many hazy and cloudy diamonds. Consequently, several other tests should be applied before concluding the stone is an imitation.

♦ The stone is checked for scratches and scraped or rounded facet edges. Diamonds are about 90 times harder than the next hardest gemstones, ruby and sapphire. This means that they generally have fewer scratches and sharper edges and corners than imitations. However, if a diamond has had much abuse or has rubbed against other diamonds, it can also show a lot of wear.

♦ The surface of the stone is examined for mirror-like reflections. Diamonds have an almost metallic-like finish, so sometimes reflections of surrounding items such as light bulbs can be seen on the facets. The reflective capacity of the stone can also be measured with an instrument called a reflectometer.

♦ The weight of the stone can be compared to the weight of diamonds of the same size. With the exception of glass, diamonds generally weigh less than imitations of the same size. This means the diamonds will sink more slowly in heavy liquids than most imitations.

♦ The stone is x-rayed. Diamonds are extremely transparent to x-rays. Imitations aren't. Diamonds also normally fluoresce blue when exposed to x-rays.

♦ A light is directed through the stone with an instrument called a spectroscope to measure how it absorbs light. Diamonds have characteristic readings.

♦ The stone is placed under short-wave and long-wave ultraviolet light and the fluorescence is compared to that of a diamond.

Perhaps you have heard of hardness tests in which the stone is scratched with something like a carbide scriber. If the stone can't be scratched, it is assumed to be a diamond because of its exceptional hardness. Most diamond professionals would advise against using this test because of the risk of damage to the stone. It's not a necessary test and the results can be misleading. The following story illustrates this.

Several years ago, a pawnbroker in the USA was called to a bank by a government official and relative of a deceased person. They wanted him to examine a large colorless emerald-cut stone in the safe-deposit box of the deceased person and verify if it was a diamond. After a quick look with his loupe, the pawnbroker said it was definitely not a diamond. The official and relative asked the pawnbroker to explain why he thought it was an imitation because it seemed odd to put a worthless stone in a safe. He indicated that it was too good to be a diamond; and to further prove his claim, the pawnbroker took a diamond hardness point tool out of his briefcase. Pressing hard, he scratched three deep x's on the table of the stone while contending that real diamonds can't be scratched. Later on, a GIA certificate was found identifying the stone as a D flawless diamond. Needless to say, the pawnbroker was sued.

Despite the fact that diamond is the hardest substance known to man, it can be chipped and cracked by non-diamond objects. If you have any doubt, ask a professional diamond setter. He has to always be on guard against damaging diamonds with setting tools. So beware of scratch tests.

While reading this chapter, some people may understandably ask, "Why should anyone spend so much money on a diamond when so many tests are required to distinguish it from an imitation?" This is like asking, "Why should anyone buy the painting of a well-known artist when reproductions are available for so much less?" One of the main reasons is that it can be a pleasure to own the real thing. Also, significant differences do exist between diamonds and the stones that imitate them. Often, it is easy for even a layperson to see these differences. This chapter, however, had to take into consideration the cases when the differences are not readily visible.

Some people may also be asking "Why was it necessary to create diamond imitations like CZ." To them, imitation stones may just be objects of deception, and the process of stone identification may be an undesirable chore. In actuality, identifying stones can be fun and challenging. It's like being a detective.

It's true that imitation diamonds may be used to deceive people, but they also have a positive side. Some of the reasons we should be glad they exist are:

♦ Imitations allow a person who can't afford diamonds to own stones that resemble them.

♦ Because of diamond imitations, there is a greater variety of costume jewelry. Even people who can afford diamonds and gold appreciate having an alternative to diamond jewelry when they travel or walk around high risk areas.

♦ Diamond imitations indirectly contribute to keeping real diamond jewelry costs down. Jewelers and jewelry manufacturers can display and promote their jewelry using samples set with imitation stones. This lowers their insurance and liability exposure, a cost which would otherwise have to be passed on to the consumer.

♦ Diamond imitations also can give us an appreciation for the real stone. When good diamonds are compared side by side with imitations, it is much easier to notice the high brilliance and incredible transparency that only a diamond can have.

The more time you spend identifying and comparing diamonds to imitations, the faster you will become at noting the differences between them and the harder it will be for people to deceive you. You will appreciate the diamonds you already own much more, and you will be better qualified to spot good value as you shop for new diamonds.

9

Gold

Gold is everywhere around us--in the plants, in the earth, in our bodies, in the rivers and oceans, in telephone and electronic circuits. Yet it is so rare, that all the world's gold could fit into a modern oil tanker. This rarity, along with its special properties, helped create a mystical aura around gold that led ancient cultures to use it for their temples, tombs, palaces, and ornaments. Let's examine the properties that differentiate gold from other metals. This can help determine why it has been so treasured and what advantages and disadvantages it has to offer as a jewelry metal.

Gold Properties

Gold in its pure state:

♦ Does not corrode, tarnish, or rust. The gold coins and jewelry found in sunken ships are as bright and shiny as they day they were made. Gold can last forever.

♦ Can be flattened and stretched more easily than any other metal. One ounce of gold can be drawn into a wire 50 miles long or flattened into a thin sheet 10,000 times the surface area of a gold coin. Entire palaces can be covered with gold leaf using only a small amount of gold.

♦ Has a deep yellow color and a high luster. This yellow color led ancient civilizations to link gold to the sun, the giver of life. By mixing other metals with it, gold can be given a variety of colors.

♦ Has a melting point of 1063° C (1945° F). When it is alloyed (mixed) with other metals to form 14K yellow gold, the melting point is lowered to about 830° C (1525° F).

♦ Is softer than most metals. It has a hardness of 2 to 2.5 on the Mohs' scale of hardness, meaning that it can easily be scratched and scraped. Gold becomes harder when alloyed with other metals.

♦ Is heavy compared to most other metals. Pure gold is about 19.3 times heavier than water and almost twice as heavy as silver and lead. Alloying it with other metals decreases its weight. 14K yellow gold is about 13 times heavier than water.

♦ Is relatively rare and therefore expensive. More steel is poured in one hour than gold has been poured since the beginning of time.

Gold's malleability and resistance to corrosion and oxidation make it an ideal metal for jewelry, but it is not necessarily the best. Platinum is also an excellent choice for jewelry. Chapter Ten explains why.

Gold Terminology

The weight and purity of gold in a piece of jewelry such as a ring play a large role in determining its price. To better compare prices, it's helpful to understand the following terms (they have been arranged in alphabetical order for easier reference):

Electroplating
A quick and inexpensive way to make any metal look like gold. The metal object is dipped in a gold plating solution and then an electrical current is used to coat the object with a thin layer of gold. The thickness of the gold depends upon the amount and duration of the current. For a ring to be called gold electroplate (commonly stamped GEP), the gold layer must be at least 7/1,000,000 of an inch thick.

Fine Gold
Contains no other elements or metals. It's also called pure gold or 24K (24 karat) gold and has a fineness of 999.

Fineness
The amount of gold in relation to 1000 parts. For example, 750 fine gold has 750 parts (75%) gold and 250 parts of other metal(s).

Gold Filled (GF)
Refers to metal objects covered by a layer of gold using heat and pressure. The layer must be at least 10K gold and 1/20th of the total weight of the object.

Gold Plate (GP) & Gold Overlay
Basically the same as gold-filled, but the gold content can be less than one-twentieth of the total weight of the item if so marked.

Karat	A measure of gold purity. One karat is 1/24 pure, so 24 karat is pure gold. Do not confuse *karat*, the unit of gold purity, with *carat*, the unit of weight for gemstones. Sometimes *karat* is spelled *carat* outside the USA.
Ounce or Pound Avoirdupois	The weight system most commonly used in the USA for food and people and almost everything else except precious metals and gems. One pound = 16 ounces.
Pennyweight (dwt)	Used in the USA as a unit of weight for gold. Twenty pennyweight = one troy ounce. The gram is the other main unit of weight for gold.
Plumb Gold (KP)	Gold that has the same purity as the mark stamped on it. 14KP means the gold is 14K, not 13 1/2K, a deviation allowed in the past.
Pure Gold	Same as fine gold.
Solid Gold	Gold that is not hollow. A term that misleads people into thinking an object is pure 24K gold even though it can be as low as 10K.
Troy Ounce (oz t)	A unit of weight commonly used in England and the USA for gold and silver. Twelve ounces troy equal one pound troy, and one ounce troy equals twenty pennyweight.

The terms for weight are clearer in the following chart.

Weight Conversion Chart	
1 pennyweight (dwt)	= 1.555 g = 0.05 oz t = 0.055 oz av = 7.776 cts
1 troy ounce (oz t)	= 31.105 g = 1.097 oz av = 20 dwt = 155.51 cts
1 ounce avoirdupois (oz av)	= 28.3495 g = 0.911 oz t = 18.229 dwt = 141.75 cts
1 carat (ct)	= 0.2 g = 0.006 oz t = 0.007 oz av = 0.31 dwt
1 gram (g)	= 5 cts = 0.032 oz t = 0.035 oz av = 0.643 dwt

Gold purity is also easier to understand by referring to a chart.

Gold Content and Notation			
USA Karat Stamping	Parts Gold	Gold %	Europe Fineness Stamping
24K	24/24	99.9%	999
22K	22/24	91.6%	916
18K	18/24	75.0%	750
14K	14/24	58.5 or 58.3%	585 or 583
12K	12/24	50.0%	500
10K	10/24	41.7%	417

Which is Better, 14K or 18K?

Diamond rings are usually made with 14K (585) and 18K (750) gold. In Europe, they're mostly 18K and in the USA, 14K, but sometimes there is a choice. You may wonder which karatage (fineness) is better.

Because of the higher gold content, 18K rings are worth more. They usually have a brighter yellow color than 14K gold, but over a period of years, the gold can wear away because of its softness. However, if the band is not unusually thin, there is no need to worry about this.

Rings of 14K gold are less expensive, usually wear better, and hold the diamonds more securely than those made of 18K, but 14K might have a tendency to discolor or tarnish due to the lower percentage of gold and a high percentage of copper. Occasionally, the metals alloyed with 14K gold cause an allergic reaction in some people.

Whether a ring is 14K or 18K is usually not an important issue. What matters more is whether you can find a ring you like in your price range. But if you have a ring custom made, you can easily choose the percentage of the gold. Consider the above points. Then have a look at some 14K and 18K rings to see if you can tell a difference. If you can, choose the gold that looks best to you.

Real Gold or Fake?

Often, buyers assume that a ring is real gold if the gold karatage or fineness is marked on it. Since there are countries that have no laws regulating these markings, this is a false assumption. In Thailand, it's possible to find rings stamped 30K (meaning 125% gold). Even in regulated countries, officials do not have time to always verify gold content. Consequently, it's important to deal with reputable jewelers. If you prefer to buy your jewelry at flea markets or from vendors, it's advisable to learn gold detection techniques.

Three ways you can check gold are with

♦ Visual tests - based on color and gold purity markings.

♦ Acid tests - based on reactions to nitric and hydrochloric acid.

♦ Price tests - based on the current market price of gold.

Of these three ways of checking gold, the acid tests are the most reliable, but since it's dangerous and inconvenient to carry nitric and hydrochloric acid, it's helpful to know how to recognize fake gold just by looking at it. Looks, however, can be deceiving.

VISUAL TESTS:

Note the color of the piece of jewelry you're checking. **Is the color the same throughout?** If it isn't, perhaps gold plating has worn off of brass, or maybe the jewelry is part gold and part another yellow metal. For example, the front and back of a necklace may be 18K gold and the metal in between may be another cheaper metal or a lower purity of gold such as 10K. Yet the whole necklace may be stamped 18K. There are cases where jewelry is designed to be multicolored, but this is usually obvious.

Are there black or silver blotches on the piece of jewelry? If there are, it could be gold plated. It could also be dirty or accidentally spotted with rhodium (see Chapter Ten for a discussion of rhodium.) Try filing some yellow metal from an inconspicuous area. If the metal is black or silver underneath, the piece is probably gold plated. Do not file the metal if it will damage or mar the beauty of the piece of jewelry in question.

Is the gold purity or karatage marked on the piece? These marks are an indication but not proof of the gold content. Their absence doesn't mean the piece is not gold. The jeweler may have just forgotten to stamp the gold purity.

How heavy does it feel? When you're visually inspecting the ring, bounce it up in your hand and see if it feels a lot heavier or lighter than other items of gold you may have. If it does, it may either be a very low karatage of gold or an entirely different metal.

ACID TESTS:

Standard acid tests for gold are based on the fact that gold will not react to pure nitric acid, but it will react to a mixture of 1 part nitric acid and 3 parts hydrochloric acid (a solution called **aqua regia**). Copper, brass, and nickel turn green and start foaming or hissing when nitric acid is applied. Gold is the only yellow metal that does not react to nitric acid. If gold is 10K or less, it will probably show a reaction due to the higher percentage of other metals.

Aqua regia (the nitric and hydrochloric acid mixture) can also be used to estimate the gold purity because the speed at which it dissolves gold is related to the percentage of gold present. For example, 14K gold is dissolved faster than 18K gold.

To determine if a piece of jewelry is 14K or 18K, rub it on a black stone slab such as slate or basalt to form a streak. Then make streaks with pieces of known 14K and 18K gold on the same slab. Apply a drop of aqua regia to each of the streaks. Compare the time it takes for the gold to disappear. If the unknown streak disappears faster than the 14K or 18K streaks, it might be 10K. If it disappears at the same rate as the 14K streak it probably is 14K. If it disappears at the same rate as the 18K streak, the tests suggests 18K gold.

Gold testing acid kits with written instructions can be purchased at jewelry supply stores. If you decide to buy one, have the salesperson demonstrate how to use it. Pay close attention to the safety precautions and never store or use the kit near children because the acids are very caustic. Pure nitric acid is so dangerous that most jewelry supply stores refuse to include it with their testing kits. It is advisable for people unaccustomed to handling acids to have their jeweler perform these tests when they want to check their gold jewelry.

PRICE TESTS:

If someone tries to sell you gold jewelry at an unbelievably low price, be suspicious. The jewelry may be gold plated, it may be of a lower fineness or karatage than marked, or it may be made of pieces of gold soldered to another cheaper metal.

You may be wondering how one can know if the price is too low or too high. To determine this, it helps to understand how gold jewelry is priced. First let's see how to calculate the value of the gold in a piece of jewelry.

Suppose an 18K (75% gold) ring weighs five pennyweight (1/4 oz t) and that the spot price for gold is $400 per ounce. The value of the gold in the ring is $75. This can be determined by first calculating the gold value of an ounce of 18K gold and by multiplying the result by 1/4 oz, the weight of the ring.

$400 x 75% = $300 worth of gold in 1 oz of 18K gold
$300 x 1/4 oz = $75 worth of gold in the ring

The price can also be determined by calculating the price per pennyweight of 18K gold. To arrive at this figure, divide $300 by 20 (20 dwt = 1 oz t), then multiply the result by 5 pennyweight, the weight of the ring.

$400 x 75% = $300 per 1 oz 18K gold

$$\frac{\$300}{20 \text{ dwt}} = \$15 \text{ per dwt}$$

$15 x 5 dwt = $75 worth of gold in the ring.

If the weight of the ring is indicated in grams, the price per gram can be determined by dividing $300 by 31.105 (1 oz t = 31.105 g).

Saying that the gold value of a ring mounting is $75 can mislead people into thinking that they can buy and sell it for $75. This is not true. If they were to sell it, money would be deducted to pay for service charges, for assaying expenses (breaking it down into its metal components), and possibly for an estimated 2% gold loss (gold starts evaporating when it is melted). If people were to buy the ring mounting, they would also pay for a retail markup, for the metals alloyed with the gold, and for the labor costs of designing, casting, and polishing the ring. It is normal for the **wholesale** cost of a mounting to be 200% and 300% more than the actual cost of the gold. The wholesale cost of custom-made and hand-crafted jewelry can be 400% and much more than the actual cost of the gold. The retailer has to naturally make a profit over these wholesale costs.

This means that people who are interested in buying gold only as an investment should buy gold coins or bars, not gold jewelry. However, gold jewelry is not a waste of money. Instead of thinking of it as a means of wearing ones investment portfolio, people should look upon gold jewelry as an opportunity to own a very special metal, an object of beauty and value which can be handed down from one generation to another.

Gold Colors

Gold in its pure state only comes in one color--yellow. However, it is possible to buy it in a variety of colors, including pink and green. Some colors of gold, such as blue, black, and purple are not easy to find, but they can be produced by mixing other metals with the gold in prescribed proportions. You are probably more familiar with white gold. It is usually a mixture of gold, copper, nickel, and zinc. Occasionally, palladium, platinum, manganese, or tin are used to make it white. Even when these metals are added, white gold may still have a yellowish cast, especially if it is 18K. The yellowish cast is not apparent, when the jewelry piece is finished because white gold is routinely plated with rhodium, a metal that gives it a hard, bright, white finish.

The next time you're in a jewelry store, ask to see some multicolored gold and note the way interesting designs and effects can be created by using more than one color. Then you will understand why multicolored gold is becoming increasingly popular. As you look, you may wonder how these different colors of gold are made. If so, you can refer to the following chart on the composition of different colored gold alloys. It's based on an article entitled "A Jeweler's Guide to Gold in Technicolor" by Tom Arnold in the December 1984 issue of *The Goldsmith*. These are not the only possible formulas for these colors.

GOLD ALLOYS:

Bright yellow, 18K (750):
   75% pure gold, 15.5% copper, 9.5% fine silver.

Bright yellow, 14K (585):
   58.5% pure gold, 29% copper, 12.5% fine silver.

White, 14K (585):
   58.3% pure gold, 23.5% copper, 12.2% nickel, 5.97% zinc.

Deep green, 18K (750):
   75% pure gold, 25% fine silver.

Deep pink, 18K (750):
   75% pure gold, 25% copper.

The following alloys are seldom made into jewelry because they are very difficult to work with.

Bright red, 18K (750) (usually brittle):
   75% pure gold, 25% aluminum.

Blue, 18K (750):
   75% pure gold, 25% iron.

Black, 14K (585):
   58.3% pure gold, 41.7% iron.

Purple, 18K (750):
   75% pure gold, 23% aluminum, 5% tin, 1.5% thorium.

White Gold or Yellow Gold?

For many people, the choice between white or yellow gold is an easy one. They choose the color they like the best and that matches the rest of their jewelry. Some people, however, have no preference and want to know which color would look best with their diamond(s). If they have a colorless or near colorless diamond, white gold or platinum would be a better choice. Yellow gold can make a colorless diamond look slightly yellowish and therefore, less valuable. Some yellow gold mountings have prongs or heads that look white. These heads are either made of white gold or platinum, or else they have been plated with rhodium. The white head compliments the color of the diamonds they hold and allows people to have yellow gold mountings that go well with colorless diamonds.

Yellow gold is ideal for mounting yellowish diamonds because it can mask their yellowish tints. If a diamond is so yellow that it can be classified as a fancy color, a white gold or platinum mounting would be more appropriate. The white metal would emphasize the yellow of the diamond.

White gold tends to be harder than yellow gold, so it can wear better and hold diamonds more securely than yellow gold. It also tends to be more brittle due to the presence of nickel. This means that when a diamond has to be removed, white gold prongs are more susceptible to breakage. The hardness and brittleness of the gold are minor factors, however, in determining the choice of color. It's far more important that you like the color and that it enhance the appearance of your diamonds.

Chapter Nine Quiz

Select the correct answer(s). **More than one answer may be possible and therefore required.**

1. You have a 14K yellow gold ring that discolors very easily. What does this indicate?

    a. The ring is not gold, because gold does not tarnish.
    b. You do not know how to take care of jewelry.
    c. The 14K gold alloy may contain a high percentage of copper.
    d. You have a cheap ring.

2. A dark pink bracelet is displayed in the window of a jewelry store with a sign saying, *14K gold bracelet, only $699*. What should you conclude?

    a. A dark pink dye was added to the gold when the bracelet was cast.
    b. The bracelet was made in Red China.
    c. The 14K gold alloy probably contains a high percentage of copper.
    d. The bracelet can't be gold so the jewelry store should be reported for fraudulent advertising.

3. In terms of actual gold value, which of the following rings is a better value if their price is the same?

    a. 14K ring weighing 5 grams.
    b. 18K ring weighing 5 grams.
    c. 14K ring weighing 5 pennyweight.
    d. 18k ring weighing 5 pennyweight.

4. You have an E color diamond and you would like to emphasize its lack of color. What type of mounting would be appropriate?

    a. A white gold mounting.
    b. A platinum mounting.
    c. A mounting entirely of yellow gold.
    d. A mounting with a white gold and/or rhodium plated head securing the diamond.

5. White gold is:

   a. A special variety of gold found only in certain mines of South Africa and Canada.
   b. Gold alloyed with silver.
   c. Gold to which bleach has been added.
   d. None of the above.

6. An 18K gold solitaire ring set with a five-carat diamond weighs six grams. What is the value of the gold if the spot price of gold is $500 per ounce.

   a. $60
   b. $65.63
   c. $72
   d. $80

7. You see *583* stamped on the inside of a ring. This number means:

   a. The ring should be 14K gold.
   b. The price of the ring is $583.
   c. The ring weighs 0.583 oz t.
   d. The ring should contain about 58% gold and 42% other metals.

8. An 18K gold bracelet weighs 1 ounce on a postage scale, one used for weighing letters. The spot price of gold is $400 an ounce. What is the value of the gold in the bracelet?

   a. $400
   b. $364.40
   c. $300
   d. $273.30

Answers

1. c

2. c

3. d. A pennyweight is 1.555 times heavier than a gram and 18K has a higher percentage of gold than 14K.

4. a,b, & d, but a or b would best satisfy your objective.

5. d. Silver is not used to make white gold. It is made by alloying yellow gold with nickel, zinc, and copper or palladium or platinum.

6. a. The diamond in the ring weighs five carats which equals 1 gram. This means the ring mounting by itself weighs 5 grams. 1 gram = 0.032 oz t, so the mounting, which weighs 5 grams = .16 oz t. Pure gold is $500 an ounce. (Remember, the weight of gold is always quoted in troy ounces). Therefore, the gold value of 18K (75%) is $375 an ounce. $375 x .16 oz t = $60

7. a and d

8. d. Remember the ounce on a postal scale is different than the ounce on a gold scale. Therefore, you'll have to convert the weight to troy ounces. 1 oz av = .911 oz t so the bracelet weighs .911 oz t. If gold is $400 an ounce, then the gold in 18K gold is worth $300 an ounce. $300 x .911 oz t = $273.30

10

Platinum

In most countries, diamonds are usually mounted in gold. Japan, however, is an exception. It's estimated that over 90% of all wedding and engagement rings sold in Japan are of platinum. In fact, 75% of all platinum jewelry in the world is bought by the Japanese. To understand why this metal is so prized in Japan, it's helpful to examine some of its characteristics.

Platinum Characteristics

Platinum:

♦ Does not corrode, tarnish, or rust.

♦ Can be easily flattened and worked in its pure state, but not as easily as gold. It becomes much harder to work with when mixed with the metal, iridium, its most common alloy in jewelry.

♦ Has a melting point of 1773° C. (3224° F.), about 1.65 times higher than that of gold.

♦ Is harder than gold and silver, so it outwears them and is not as easily scratched. It's hardness is 4 to 4.5 on Mohs' scale of hardness, about the same as iron. When platinum is mixed with iridium, it becomes much harder and therefore more suitable for jewelry wear.

♦ Has a grayish-white or steel color. It shines well but is not as reflective as gold or silver.

♦ Is very heavy compared to other metals. It's 21.45 times heavier than water, about twice as heavy as silver, about 1.65 times heavier than 14 karat gold, and about 1.4 times heavier than 18 karat gold. Mixing platinum with 10% iridium makes it only slightly heavier.

♦ Is very rare and expensive, even more so than gold. The major sources are South Africa, Canada, the U.S.S.R, and Colombia. (For a short time in 1991, however, the price of platinum did fall below that of gold. This occurred only two other times during the previous 15 years).

Related Metals and Platinum Purity

You may hear about the five other metals that are part of the platinum family--iridium, rhodium, ruthenium, palladium, and osmium--and you may wonder how they relate to jewelry. **Rhodium** is used to plate white gold and platinum because it is harder and more reflective. It's also used to make yellow gold look like white gold and to prevent silver from tarnishing. **Iridium** (5% to 15%) is usually mixed with platinum to make it harder and more suitable for jewelry wear. **Ruthenium** is occasionally used to harden platinum. **Palladium** is relatively inexpensive and lightweight so it is occasionally used to reduce the cost and weight of platinum. It is also mixed with gold to form white or brown gold and, at times, has been used alone to imitate white gold. **Osmium** is the hardest metal known and is rarely used in jewelry.

Platinum jewelry is identified by the marks **PT, pt, plat**, or **platinum**. To be called platinum, the metal must consist of at least 85% platinum (many countries such as the USA, Hong Kong, and England require 90% or 95% platinum). If the purity is less than 85%, then the other metals and their percentages have to be identified when calling metal *platinum*.

A percentage marking is common even when the platinum content is 85% or more. Percentage markings are made as follows:

PT 950	95% platinum
PT 900	90% platinum
PT 850	85%platinum
5% RUTH PT	5% ruthenium, 95% platinum
5% IRID PT	5% iridium, 95% platinum
10% IRID PT	10% iridium, 90% platinum

White Gold or Platinum?

The question above can be interpreted two different ways: Should you buy white gold or platinum or is the metal you are looking at white gold or platinum? Let's first compare the differences between them.

PLATINUM	**WHITE GOLD (WG)**
Almost twice as heavy as most 14K gold alloys so is more durable	Lighter than platinum
More expensive mainly due to its higher purity	Less expensive than platinum, slightly more expensive than yellow gold
Wears better and holds diamonds more securely than gold due to its strength, hardness, and density	14K and 18K nickel white gold is harder than platinum and yellow gold. It's not as dense or strong as platinum
Fewer styles to choose from than gold	More ring styles to choose from than platinum, fewer than yellow gold
More difficult to find a qualified person to repair rings of platinum because it requires special expertise	Most experienced jewelers can repair white gold rings.

You might wonder why it is so difficult to find jewelers qualified to make and repair platinum rings. One of the main reasons is the high melting point of platinum--about twice that of 14K and 18K gold. Casting platinum is particularly difficult because, unlike gold, platinum solidifies almost instantly, which makes speed and timing very important. Even when a jeweler knows how to work with and cast platinum, he may not have the special equipment needed for it.

The extra work and expertise required for handling platinum naturally increases the price of platinum rings. They can be almost double the cost of gold rings even though the price of platinum may be from 5% to 25% higher than gold (in 1992 platinum ranged from about $345 to $380 an ounce, whereas in 1990 platinum ranged from about $420 to $550 an ounce). The higher weight and purity of platinum as well as the higher cost of the alloying metals also contribute to the increased cost.

Let's return to the question of **should you buy a white gold or platinum ring**. The answer depends mainly on your budget, the style ring you want, and where you live. If you want a simple, elegant ring and money is no issue, then you would probably be better off with a platinum ring, unless you have no access to a city where platinum jewelers could be found. If you have limited funds or the style you want is not available in platinum, then white gold would be best. You might also consider having a gold ring with platinum prongs. It's hard to tell the difference between a platinum and white gold ring by appearance alone because both are routinely plated with the metal, rhodium, to give them a brighter, whiter look.

Rhodium plating can also be done on yellow gold and silver. It can prevent the silver from tarnishing and it can make yellow gold look like white gold. Since rhodium is so hard, it does not wear away as quickly as yellow gold plating. People who are allergic to 10K or 14K gold earring posts or other types of jewelry sometimes have them plated with rhodium when they discover it helps eliminate allergic reactions.

Rhodium plating all of the metal of your ring is a quick and inexpensive process. The ring is specially cleaned. Then, for 15 to 20 seconds, it is immersed in a rhodium solution with an electrical current running through it. Afterwards, the ring is rinsed and dried. If you want your ring to be part white and part yellow, then more time is needed to cover the yellow with a special paint or masking before plating.

There might be times when you wonder, **"Is the ring white gold or platinum?"** Usually a marking on the ring will identify the metal, but this marking can be wrong. If you suspect it is, bounce the ring in your hand and judge how heavy it feels in comparison to a gold ring you have. If it feels a lot heavier and it's marked platinum, it probably is.

Jewelers and polishers usually know immediately when they start working on a ring if it's platinum because the metal is so hard and heavy. Sometimes, they do an acid test similar to the one described for gold in Chapter Nine since platinum reacts in a characteristic manner to stannous chloride solutions mixed with aqua regia (a mixture of nitric and hydrochloric acid).

Generally the easiest way for the layperson to be assured of the type of metal he's buying, is to deal with reliable jewelers. They, in turn, have to deal with reliable suppliers because they don't have time to test every piece of jewelry they sell. Finding a person you can trust is not always easy, but a general knowledge of metals and gemstones can make you a better judge of a jeweler's honesty.

Chapter Ten Quiz

True or False?

1. Platinum is an ideal metal for mounting colorless diamonds.

2. If a jeweler is qualified to work with gold, he's also qualified to work with platinum.

3. Platinum is less expensive than white gold.

4. Platinum is almost twice as heavy as most 14K gold alloys.

5. Rhodium plating is sometimes used to prevent silver from tarnishing.

6. Gold holds diamonds more securely than platinum.

7. Platinum is used to mask the color of yellowish diamonds.

8. Platinum is an excellent alternative for people who are allergic to gold alloys.

9. Platinum is harder and more durable than gold.

10. Rhodium is commonly used to plate both white gold and platinum.

11. Gold rings are never made with platinum prongs because it's impossible to solder the two metals together due to their different melting temperatures.

12. Neither pure gold nor platinum will tarnish.

Answers

1. T, 2. F, 3. F, 4. T, 5. T, 6. F, 7. F, 8. T, 9. T, 10. T, 11. F, 12. T.

11

Choosing an Appropriate Setting Style

What setting style is best for your diamond(s) and why? To answer this question, you'll need to know what styles there are to choose from and what advantages each has to offer. Described below are five basic styles:

Prong or Claw This is the most common type of setting, especially for ladies' solitaire diamond rings (fig 12.1). It involves fitting the diamond in a metal head or basket and securing it with a minimum of three prongs or metal claws. There are many decorative variations of this style. **Cluster settings** which allow diamonds to be grouped together like a bouquet of flowers, frequently use prongs to hold the stones (fig. 12.2).

Bezel or Tube A bezel is a band of metal soldered onto the mounting to surround the diamond and hold it in place. In the past, bezel settings have been used mostly for dome-shaped stones (cabochons) such as jade and star sapphire. They are being used more often now as attractive settings for diamonds (fig. 12.3).

Channel This style is often used for wedding bands. The diamonds are suspended in a channel of vertical walls with no metal separating the stones (fig. 12.4).

Fig. 12.1 Prong-set solitaire ring

Fig. 12.2 Prong-set cluster ring

Fig. 12.3 Bezel-set ring

Fig. 12.4 Channel-set ring & mounting

Fig. 12.5 Pavé-set ring

Fig. 12.6 Flush-set ring

Photo credit for figures 12.3 and 12.6: Shinsoshoku Co. Ltd, Japan.

Bead or Pave'

In this type of setting, diamonds are fit into tapered holes and set almost level with the surface of the ring (fig. 12.5). Then some of the surrounding metal is raised to form beads which hold the diamond in place. This style is frequently used for women's

When there are three or more rows of diamonds set in this way, it is called **pave'**, which, in French, means *paved* like a cobblestone road. The jewelry trade often refers to any type of bead setting as pave'. In order to give the impression of a continuous diamond surface, it is customary to use white gold metal to support pave'-set diamonds even if the rest of the mounting is yellow gold. Rhodium plating is added to further heighten this effect. If diamonds are yellowish, they tend to look better set in yellow gold without rhodium plating.

Flush or Gypsy

Flush setting is a popular style for men's rings. The diamond is fit snugly into a tapered hole that is grooved to hold the girdle of the stone. Then the surrounding metal is pressed and hammered around the rim of the opening to secure the diamond (fig. 12.6). In a gypsy ring mounting, a center stone is set in a moderate to high dome at the top of the ring.

There are advantages and disadvantages to each of the above styles. Some of these are listed below:

PRONG SETTING

Positive points:

♦ Allows the maximum amount of light to enter a stone from all angles, making diamonds appear more brilliant than in other setting styles. This is why it is so popular for ladies' solitaire diamond rings.

♦ Is quicker and therefore, less expensive to set than the other styles.

♦ Can hold large diamonds securely. Small diamonds (less than 0.10 ct) may fall out with hard wear because often, they are not set with the same care as a larger, more prominently displayed stone.

♦ Allows the diamonds to be more easily cleaned than the other styles--provided the prongs are not encased with a lot of metal or wire.

♦ Can be used to set any type of gemstone, no matter how fragile it is. Prong setting is particularly popular for transparent faceted gemstones.

Negative points.

♦ Does not protect diamonds as well as other styles since it leaves most of the girdle area exposed.

♦ Does not provide as smooth of a ring surface as some of the other styles. Sometimes, the prongs have a tendency to get caught in clothing and hair.

BEZEL SETTING

Positive points:

♦ Provides good protection for the girdle and pavilion areas of diamonds.

♦ When done properly, holds diamonds well.

♦ Can be used to set almost all gemstones without causing damage to them.

♦ Provides a smooth ring surface.

Negative Point:

♦ Is usually more time consuming and expensive than prong and bead setting.

CHANNEL SETTING

Positive points:

♦ Protects the girdle area of the diamonds.

♦ When done properly, secures small diamonds better than bead or prong setting.

♦ Provides a smooth ring surface.

♦ Is appropriate for enhancing ring shanks and for creating linear designs with a tailored look.

Negative points:

♦ Is usually more time consuming and expensive than prong setting. Square or rectangular diamonds cost more than round diamonds to channel set.

♦ Is a very risky setting method, in terms of damage to stones, so should not be used for fragile gems.

BEAD OR PAVE SETTING

Positive points:

♦ Protects diamonds better than prong setting.

♦ Allows uninterrupted designs of varying width. When these pavé designs are spread over the surface of a mounting, they can make the diamonds look larger and more numerous than they actually are.

Negative points:

♦ Is a risky setting method in terms of possible stone damage. Good diamonds, rubies, and sapphires can withstand the pressure of being pavé set, but fragile stones such as emeralds, opals, tourmalines, and diamonds with large cracks risk damage.

♦ Does not provide as smooth of a ring surface as bezel, channel, and flush setting.

♦ May not be as secure as other settings.

FLUSH OR GYPSY SETTING

Positive points:

♦ Protects the girdle area of diamonds.

♦ When done properly, holds diamonds well.

♦ Provides a smooth, tailored look.

Negative points:

♦ Is usually more time consuming and expensive than prong and bead setting.

♦ Is a very risky setting method, in terms of damage to stones, so should not be used for fragile gems.

An awareness of the benefits and drawbacks of the various setting styles can be helpful in choosing diamond jewelry. To see how, let's look at the following examples:

♦ Sandy is active in contact sports and is hard on jewelry. Her funds are limited so she can only afford small diamonds. She wants a diamond ring that would be suitable for everyday wear.

Sandy might consider buying a sturdy channel-set ring. The ring could be very smooth so it wouldn't scratch other players if she forgot to take it off during a game, and there would not be as much risk of the small diamonds falling out due to broken prongs or beads. Despite the increased setting costs, the ring price should be a lot less than one with a large diamond of the same total weight and quality.

♦ Pierre is a construction engineer. He wants a diamond wedding ring that he can wear as much as possible.

Pierre might consider choosing a sturdy flush-set diamond ring with a matte or florentine (crosshatched) finish. Scratches would not show up as easily with these finishes, and the low, flush setting could help protect his diamond from the unusual abuse it might get if he didn't want to take it off during work. Gypsy, bezel- or channel-set rings could also be suitable, but he should avoid high prongs.

♦ Charlene is looking for a dinner ring with lots of flash. She does not have enough money for a large diamond.

Charlene might consider getting a pavé- or cluster-set diamond ring. Even with small diamonds, it could display an impressive, sparkling mass of brilliance.

It's not common practice for jewelry buyers to analyze what setting styles would be best and why, but it should be. Too often, jewelry that looks attractive when bought turns out to be impractical. With a bit of forethought, it's possible to select a style that is not only aesthetically pleasing but functional as well.

12

Choosing A Diamond Ring

The Significance of the Diamond Ring

Think of a circle. It has no beginning or end. Think of a knot tied around your finger. It binds and reminds. And so it is with a ring. It reminds you of an eternal binding commitment to a lover, spouse, friend, school, church, club, or country.

The commitment to marry a woman is usually expressed by placing a ring on her fourth finger. This custom might have originated with the Egyptians. They believed a special vein or nerve ran from that finger to the heart. Another explanation for the custom is that it may have been a suggestion to women that they should be submissive to their future husbands since the fourth finger is the weakest one and can't be used independently. A third explanation is that placing the ring on the fourth finger may have been a way to avoid damaging the ring since it is the best-protected finger.

Diamonds were probably first added to wedding and engagement rings in the 15th century. To the upper class Europeans of this period, diamonds represented fortitude, innocence, prosperity, and faithfulness. They assumed that a diamond's power to withstand natural forces could be transferred to the owners and that they, in turn, would be able to withstand temptation and adversity. Religious and cultural beliefs outside of Europe also contributed to the mystique of the diamond. The Hindus felt that offering a diamond to Krishna was a guarantee of eternal life in the highest heaven. Buddhists used the diamond as a symbol of spiritual balance, peace of mind, clarity of thought, and unlimited insight.

A ring rather than a pin, necklace, earring, or bracelet is traditionally used as a pledge of marriage. As already mentioned, the circular ring symbolizes an eternal commitment of love. In addition, it can be worn anytime anywhere without getting in the way, and you don't need a mirror to enjoy it.

Choosing a Ring Style

Many people choose a ring style only on the basis of how pretty it looks, and this is normal. However, they should also ask if the ring is:

♦ Flattering to their hand
♦ Suitable for their needs
♦ Comfortable
♦ Worth the price

In this chapter, the term **mounting** will often be used instead of *ring style*. This is the term that the jewelry trade uses for rings before they are set with stones. Previous chapters have already suggested how to choose the shape of your diamond(s) and the setting style, so this chapter will be limited to the choice of mounting.

No matter how practical or valuable a ring is, there's no point in buying it if you don't like the style. Therefore, unless you buy and sell jewelry for profit, you should naturally select a style that is attractive to you. When making your choice, ask yourself too if the mounting enhances the diamonds and if it will probably be in style in ten or twenty years.

Even though a ring may look attractive to you, it may not flatter your hand. **Do you have a small hand and short fingers?** A huge broad ring can make your fingers look too short and your hand too small. To make your fingers look longer, you can choose a mounting with stones or lines arranged diagonally across or down the length of your finger. Otherwise you might wear simple rings with thin bands.

Do you have long thin fingers? Button and cluster styles and large broad rings can look good on your hands. A mounting with stones or lines flowing across your finger or that have height can make your hand look shorter.

Do you have long broad hands? A very small ring will tend to make them look bigger, so normally a larger ring is better. If you're a woman, simple or delicate designs should flatter your hand.

Do you have an average-size hand? You're fortunate. Almost any ring will look good on your hand. However, a ring that is too large can make your hand look smaller and defeat the advantage of having an ideal-size hand.

Besides flattering your hand, a ring should be **suitable for your needs**. If it's for everyday or business wear, a simple style will probably be best. If it's for dress, you might want something fancier. No matter where you intend to wear your ring, there are some practical things to consider for it to be suitable. When choosing a ring, ask yourself the following questions:

♦ Does the mounting have points and sharp edges which could cut you or damage your clothing or furniture? Often the points can be rounded off and the sharp edges filed or polished away, but sometimes there is nothing you can do to prevent a mounting from snagging your clothes.

♦ Is it easy to clean, especially if it's for everyday wear?

♦ Does it blend in with your other jewelry, if you plan to wear them together?

♦ If the ring is for everyday wear, will scratches on the mounting be very noticeable? If so, you may wish to either choose another mounting or else have a matte, brushed, or florentine (crosshatched) finish added to the mounting you like.

♦ Is the band so thin that it will wear down quickly if you wear it everyday? If you can bend the band easily with your fingers, it's probably too thin.

♦ Can the ring be sized easily? Does your weight or finger size change frequently? If so, pay attention to the sizing factor and avoid, for example, eternity rings that have stones all around the band. Instead choose a ring where at least one third of the band is unset metal. If you think your finger size could change by two or more sizes (this is unlikely), mention this to your jeweler and he will help you select an appropriate mounting. He'll probably suggest that you avoid rings with lots of baguette-shaped stones set up and down the sides of the mounting.

♦ If you live in a cold climate and need to wear gloves, can you slip them on without damaging your ring or ripping the gloves?

♦ Does your center diamond always flop to the side, or does the ring stay in an attractive position as your hand moves? This problem sometimes occurs when a large diamond is mounted on a ring. It can be corrected by choosing a wider band or a band that is square or oval in shape instead of round. This problem can also occur if the ring is too big.

Some of these practical considerations may not apply to you because of your special needs. The author knows of one man that wanted a ring to serve as a weapon. He had it designed as a pyramid coming to a sharp point on top in order to enable him to rip the skin of an attacker as he punched him in the face. Liberace had a ring designed to look like a piano. Even if Liberace had lived in a cold climate, it wouldn't have mattered if gloves would fit over it.

Ring comfort may seem to be a matter of common sense. Yet many people ignore this factor, particularly when they buy rings through mail-order or have them custom made. When choosing a ring ask yourself:

♦ Can you bend your fingers easily when wearing it? If not, the band may be too wide. Besides being uncomfortable, it could cause skin irritation due to collection of moisture and dirt under the band. If you like the wide-, broad-ring look, select a band that tapers down from a wide top to a narrow bottom so that your finger can bend freely.

♦ Does your ring fit between your fingers without feeling cumbersome or forcing your hand into a spread eagle position?

♦ Is the ring too tight or too loose? This can be corrected by resizing the ring. If your band is more than 3/8" (10 mm.) wide, it will probably need to be a half size larger than what you normally wear in order to feel comfortable.

♦ Does the inside of the ring feel rough and scratchy? If the metal band does, it can be smoothed down by polishing. Occasionally, diamonds are set too low and the pointed bottoms prick your finger. If this is the case, it would probably be easier to choose another ring than to correct the problem.

♦ Does the ring feel too bulky and heavy, or are you able to forget that you're wearing it?

Once you have decided that a ring is attractive, suitable, and comfortable, you might wonder if it's **worth the price**. To determine this, you need to know the factors which affect the cost of mountings, and to understand these factors you should know the following terms:

Cast	Refers to mountings made by thrusting molten metal into plaster of paris type molds with a centrifugal force or vacuum. The mold is made by pouring the plaster of paris type material over a wax model of the desired ring. The wax is then melted, leaving a ring mold.
	Casting is a relatively fast process that allows many identical articles to be made from a single design, which is why most jewelry is cast. Cast mountings are relatively porous and therefore less durable than those that are handmade or die-struck.
Die-struck	Refers to mountings formed with metal parts mechanically punched out of compressed sheet metal with dies (forms or molds). Since this metal is harder and more compact than cast metal, it is less subject to wear. Die-struck mountings generally have simple, standard designs and are produced in large quantities.

Hand-fabricated   Refers to mountings made by sawing, filing, and shaping metal parts and wire by hand and then soldering them together. A hand-fabricated mounting is literally *one of a kind* and takes a lot of time to make.

Custom-made   Made for special order instead of mass-produced. Generally, *custom-made* refers to rings requiring handwork or individual casting and specially-made molds. It can also refer to rings formed by soldering pre-fabricated metal parts together to form a design chosen by a customer. If a customer has a ring modified by changing the stones, it is usually called a **remount**.

Factors Affecting the Cost of Mountings

♦ The higher the gold or platinum content the greater the cost of the mounting. Therefore the weight of a mounting is an important cost factor.

♦ The value of the metal in the mounting increases as follows: 14 karat gold < 18 karat gold < platinum.

♦ Sometimes, white gold mountings cost slightly more than those of yellow gold because they are often made to order. Also, since white gold is alloyed with nickel, it is a harder metal to work, which may add to the labor cost.

♦ Mountings engraved with the name of the designer or jeweler usually cost more than those without such an engraving.

♦ Mountings that require a lot of work to cast, shape, or polish cost more than those that are quick and easy to finish.

♦ Hand-fabricated mountings cost more than cast and die-struck mountings.

♦ Custom-made mountings cost more than mass-produced mountings. If a jeweler has to make a mold and cast a ring individually, you can expect to pay at least double what it would have cost if it had been mass produced.

When you evaluate the cost of ring mountings, keep all the above factors in mind. Try to compare mountings of the same metal, weight, and manufacturing process. Slight differences in mountings do not normally affect the cost of a diamond ring very much. In most cases, the major portion of the cost is in the diamonds. Slight, unnoticeable differences in diamond quality can have a large effect on the cost of a diamond ring.

Tips on Buying Custom-made Rings

If you're unable to find a ready-made diamond ring that's attractive, comfortable, and suitable for your needs, you might try having one custom made. Not only will your ring be unique, it will probably mean more to you if you participate in creating it.

Having a ring made to order should be a positive experience, and you can help prevent it from turning into a disappointing one by taking the following precautions:

♦ Try on rings that resemble the one you want to have made. What looks good in a picture may not look or feel good on your hand.

♦ If possible, have good drawings, photos, or models of the ring you want made. Never assume that the jeweler understands your verbal description of what you want.

♦ Don't assume a ring will look exactly like it does in a photo. It should however have a close resemblance. The best way to get exactly what you want is to have a model or a sample ring.

♦ Be as specific as possible about ring features that you consider important. For example, state in advance if you want the prongs holding your diamonds to be rounded off or hammered in a square or triangular form. Otherwise, the jeweler will assume that the prong style doesn't matter to you so long as the prongs are secure and uniform and don't cover too much of the diamonds. You should also tell the jeweler beforehand if you want the inside of your ring to have a special look. In one instance, a lady wanted thin bars under every stone of a diamond eternity band instead of under every other stone. Unless jewelers are told otherwise, they will probably assume that as long as the inside of a ring is smooth and well polished, its appearance won't matter much to a customer since the inside doesn't show when the ring is worn.

♦ If you have a ring that fits well and has about the same band width as the custom ring you are ordering, show it to the salesperson or jeweler so they can choose the best ring size for you. The sample metal rings they have you try on can sometimes suggest the wrong size.

♦ Always tell a jeweler you need the ring earlier than you actually do, especially if it's a complicated job. Work out an acceptable delivery date and have it put in writing. But still be prepared for delays. It's best not to rush custom-made jewelry.

♦ If possible, avoid having jewelry custom made in December in countries that celebrate Christmas. Since jewelers are rushed and overworked at that time of year, they might not do their best work then.

♦ Get a written estimate of the cost of the ring. If more diamonds are needed than estimated, the jeweler is not expected to give them to you free of charge. He should, however, get your permission before doing anything that would increase the estimated cost of the ring.

♦ Know in advance who will be responsible if your diamonds are lost or damaged during setting or recutting. If you give a jeweler your diamonds, he is not always liable if something unfortunate happens to them. Reliable jewelers, however, will either feel morally obligated to replace damaged or lost diamonds or else will clearly warn you that your diamonds are at risk.

♦ Know the refund policy of the jeweler. It is normal for jewelers to retain at least a portion of your deposit if you decide not to buy the ring you ordered, particularly if it's a style that would be difficult to sell.

♦ Develop a relationship with a jeweler you can trust. Then you won't have to worry about having unpleasant surprises when you have jewelry custom made.

13

Judging Craftsmanship

You can find fault with any piece of diamond jewelry if you look hard enough. Somewhere there will be a little pit, scratch, unevenness, or lack of symmetry. If these deviations are so obvious that they detract from the beauty of the piece, then the craftsmanship can be classified as unacceptable. Judging craftsmanship is more a matter of assessing the overall effect of a piece than of adding up all of its minor defects.

Good craftsmanship entails a variety of skills. Just making a simple-looking diamond ring can be a complex, time-consuming process. The major steps involved are:

♦ Designing the ring

♦ Making the mounting

♦ Picking the diamonds for the ring

♦ Setting the diamonds

♦ Polishing and/or plating the ring

Since each step requires different skills, it is normal for several people to be involved in making a ring. If the ring is cheap and of low quality, these steps may be carried out as fast as possible by low-paid, poorly skilled workers.

Perhaps you're wondering how you can recognize a low-quality ring. Even though there are no formal written standards for jewelry craftsmanship, most jewelers would agree that the characteristics described in the following section indicate poor craftsmanship. For the sake of clarity, they are organized in terms of four of the manufacturing steps (design and style were already discussed in Chapter Twelve).

Poor Craftsmanship

The mounting is poorly made if, with the naked eye, you can easily see:

♦ **Large noticeable pits and bumps** in the gold or platinum that give the mounting a miniature swiss cheese look. Besides looking bad, lots of holes can mean the metal is not as strong as it should be (fig. 13.1).

♦ **Solder joints.** Your ring should look like one continuous piece of metal, not like pieces joined together.

♦ **Variations in gold color.** Occasionally, patterns are intentionally formed by different colors of gold, but normally the color of the gold should be the same throughout the ring.

♦ **Crooked and unsymmetrical mounting parts**. Is the metal head holding the center stone tilted or off to the side of the ring? Does the right side of the ring look the same as the left side if they are supposed to look the same? Hopefully, your ring will have a balanced and well-proportioned look.

The diamonds are poorly picked if:

♦ You can see **obvious color differences in the diamonds** with your naked eye. Occasionally, the color of the center or major diamonds are intentionally different from the other diamonds, but normally all the diamonds are supposed to blend together.

♦ **The diamonds are much too large or too small for their settings.**

♦ With your naked eye, you can see **obvious differences in the clarity and cutting quality of diamonds.** For example, it's pointless to pay a high price for high quality VS diamonds and mix them with low quality I_2 diamonds.

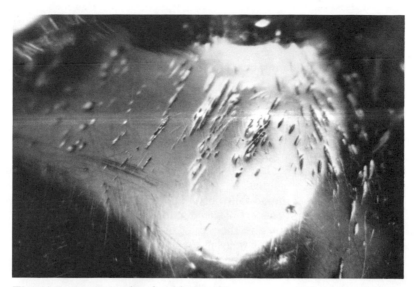

Fig. 13.1 An example of gold porosity

Fig. 13.2 An example of poor setting. Note how irregular and different in size and shape the prongs are.

The diamonds are poorly set if:

♦ With the unaided eye, it's obvious that **the prongs or beads holding the diamonds are of different shapes, sizes, and styles** (fig. 13.2).

♦ **You can hardly see the diamonds** because they are covered by so much metal from the beads, prongs, or bezel.

♦ **The diamonds are loose and move around.** This is a fairly common problem and, usually, it's easily corrected. If setters put too much pressure on a diamond, it can chip or crack, so sometimes they go to the other extreme and don't secure stones well enough. Once you start wearing a ring and knocking it about, do not expect the diamonds to remain secure. You should have them checked at least every six months or whenever you hear your ring rattle or click as it is shaken or as a diamond is tapped next to your ear. It would be unreasonable to blame a jeweler when a diamond falls out of your ring a year after you buy it.

You can expect rings with clusters of tiny diamonds to start losing their stones a couple months after you buy them if you give them a lot of everyday abuse such as knocking them on counters, dishes, and furniture or wearing them in hot tubs where they expand and then contract. Therefore, you should either reserve such rings for special occasions or else have them frequently checked.

A ring is poorly polished or plated if:

♦ **The inside of the ring is rough and unpolished.**

♦ **The outside of the ring has sharp and rough edges or points** that cut you or rip your clothing.

♦ **The metal securing your diamonds is polished away.**

♦ With the naked eye **you can see silver-colored spots or lines** on the yellow-gold portion of the ring. This sometimes occurs when rings are rhodium plated.

♦ **The ring looks obviously dull, old, or dirty,** yet it's brand new.

If you find a ring that is just what you want but that has one of the above problems, ask to have it corrected and feel confident that you are making a reasonable request.

Perhaps you wish to go beyond spotting unacceptable work and would like to recognize top-quality craftsmanship. While reading the discussion of this in the next section, you should realize that you may never find a ring that meets all of the criteria outlined below. In fact, people that insist on these standards of craftsmanship could be considered over-critical, unless they are willing to pay premium prices.

Superior Craftsmanship

A mounting is exceptionally well-made if:

♦ **The metal looks perfectly smooth through a ten-power magnifier.** Rarely can one find a cast mounting that under ten-power magnification does not show at least one or two tiny pits or pores (a condition called porosity).

Porosity can result from cooling the ring too slowly, from casting too many rings together, from using either remelted or the wrong quality gold alloys, or from not maintaining consistent and proper temperatures in the mold and the metal. The list of reasons for porosity can go on, which is why most cast jewelry has at least a trace of porosity. As long as it isn't obvious, there's no need to worry about microscopic porosity.

One way of avoiding porosity is to buy a die-struck mounting, made of metal parts mechanically punched out of sheet metal. But even then, porosity may be present around its solder joints.

♦ **Under ten-power magnification all parts of the mounting look symmetrical,** if they are intended to look that way.

♦ **The metal is a high quality alloy (metal mixture) and has not been remelted too many times.** There is no easy way for a layperson to determine this. Jewelers and setters will suspect a metal problem if it seems too weak or brittle when they work with it. Creating an ideal alloy is an art. It requires an in-depth knowledge of metallurgy as well as a great deal of experience.

♦ **Intricate designs may have been tastefully carved in the mounting.** Such work will involve extra labor cost.

The diamonds have been exceptionally well-picked if:

♦ **The height, width, and length measurements of the diamonds are the same** where they are intended to look the same. Diamonds of exactly the same size are often impossible to find. Consequently, when large diamonds or several small diamonds have to be matched for size, it is normal for their measurements to differ by a couple hundredths of a millimeter.

♦ **The table size, the crown height, the pavilion depth, and the girdle thickness of the diamonds are the same.** A group of diamonds meeting these standards would be so difficult to find that you should be amazed if you come across them.

♦ **Under ten-power magnification the diamonds appear to have the same color and clarity grades.** Normally, one has to be content with diamonds of just similar quality.

♦ **The diamonds fit their settings perfectly.** Often one has to compromise on the size of the diamonds in favor of the color or clarity.

It's possible to spend days and months searching the world to find diamonds that look exactly alike and still not find them. To be so exacting can be a waste of time and money. What counts is that the diamonds blend together well. Finding diamonds of a carat or more in weight that look even approximately the same can be a problem, so you should expect to pay more for a matched pair of diamonds than for unmatched ones.

The diamonds are exceptionally well-set if:

♦ **Under ten-power magnification the prongs and beads all look the same size and shape** and have an aesthetically pleasing appearance.

♦ **All the diamonds are set horizontally (not tilted) at consistent and proper heights in their settings.** Sometimes this is impossible due to the sizes and shapes of the diamonds. To test for consistent setting, tilt the piece of jewelry and see if the the tables of all the diamonds flash at the same time.

♦ There are either **no spaces between channel set diamonds or else the spaces are of uniform size.**

♦ There is **just enough metal to hold the diamonds securely, yet display as much of the diamonds as possible.** Achieving this balance is difficult.

A ring is exceptionally well-polished if:

♦ **The metal is as smooth and reflective as a mirror** unless it has a matte or florentine finish. Then the finish should be of uniform quality.

♦ **The inside of the ring is polished as well as the outside of the ring.** There are times when it is impossible to polish inner parts of a ring. However, an exceptional polish will show that a lot of attention has been paid to detail even in hard-to-reach areas.

Jewelry craftsmanship ranges from an unacceptable level to an ideal level, with the quality of most jewelry falling somewhere in between. Due to consumer demands for inexpensive jewelry and pressure on jewelers to complete jobs as fast as possible, the quality often approaches or even falls within the unacceptable range.

It is not easy to know where to draw the line between acceptable and unacceptable craftsmanship. However, if you start examining jewelry for the good- and bad-quality characteristics listed in this chapter and comparing excellent pieces with average or poor pieces, you will develop an eye for good craftsmanship. You will know what standards of craftsmanship are reasonable and, in turn, you will be able to select high quality jewelry.

Also, you will note that a high price tag does not necessarily imply high-quality craftsmanship. It could just mean a high mark-up or a high diamond and metal value. More often than not, the major portion of the cost is for the diamond(s). Occasionally, though, an exceptional amount of time and skill are required to make a piece and the cost of the labor is greater than the cost of the materials. Don't be discouraged if you have difficulty determining what percentage of the price is for labor, metal, or the diamond(s). People in the trade even find it challenging to break down these costs. Jewelry evaluation is an art just as jewelry making is an art. Both require practice, but mastering the necessary skills of either art can bring satisfaction and lead to a greater appreciation of jewelry.

14

Is Your Jeweler a Crook?

Jane was walking through the jewelry district in downtown Los Angeles when she spotted a store called *Diamonds Galore*. She had come from Fresno, California on a business trip and wanted to take advantage of some free time to find a diamond ring for her husband. *Diamonds Galore* had a nice selection of men's rings in their display window, so Jane went in to have a look.

Mabel, the owner, showed her a number of rings. Jane finally found one she liked, but she didn't know if it would look good on her husband. Mabel said not to worry because even if her husband didn't like it, it was such a great buy that the ring could be sold to a jeweler in Fresno for double its cost. This sounded like a good deal to Jane, so she bought the ring.

As Jane suspected, the ring wasn't what her husband wanted. She took it to some jewelers in Fresno, and the most they would give her for it was about one-third what she paid. The weight and the quality of the diamonds and gold in the ring were as Mabel described them, and the price of the ring seemed fair when compared to the retail prices of similar rings in Fresno. Nevertheless, Jane thought Mabel was a crook who had misled her into buying a ring by making false claims about its value. If this were a true story, would Jane be correct in her judgment of Mabel?

According to guidelines established by the Federal Trade Commission in the United States, Jane would be correct. Deception of any kind is a fraudulent practice, even when it involves only the future value or resale potential of jewelry. In fact, when anyone sells jewelry for purposes of financial investment, they must inform the buyer that "appreciation or profit cannot be assured" and that "no organized market exists for the resale of jewelry industry products by private owners."

129

Jewelers themselves helped write these guidelines for the jewelry industry. Ethical jewelers support laws against fraud. They want to earn the respect of the public and to be regarded as people of integrity.

Occasionally, jewelers are accused of being crooks if they have mark-ups of, for example, 100%. However, when one considers their overhead and compares jewelry mark-ups to those of goods in other industries, this seems to be an unfair accusation. How much of a mark-up is involved in a designer scarf or suit? How much of a mark-up is there on brand-name pharmaceutical products? Perhaps a lot more than one will find on jewelry. How many other industries offer trade-in allowances equal to or higher than the original purchase price when people trade in products they've used for years on brand new ones? The fact that such trade-in policies are offered on jewelry says a lot about its value in comparison to other goods.

Questions to Ask When Choosing Jewelers

There are a lot of things to consider when choosing a jeweler. It's not just a matter of finding the one that seems to have the lowest prices in town. When making your choice, consider the answers to the following questions:

♦ What kind of reputation do they have?

♦ How long have they been in business? If they're a fly-by-night operation, their guarantees won't mean much.

♦ What types of services do they offer? Can they do repairs, appraisals, custom work and designs?

♦ What types of guarantees do they offer? What are their refund, replacement, and buy-back policies?

♦ Do they contradict themselves during their sales presentations?

♦ Are they willing to put their verbal descriptions and claims in writing?

♦ When problems arise, do they try to resolve them graciously?

♦ Are they willing to let you examine their jewelry under magnification?

♦ When you are seriously interested in something, will they make an effort to find what you want even if they don't have it in stock?

♦ Do they have a range of qualities to choose from? This isn't a necessity, but it is a convenience.

♦ Is their merchandise always on sale with the same discount? If they try to mislead you with phony sales, they might try to mislead you in other ways.

♦ Do they try to discredit the competition? Competent jewelers don't need to resort to such tactics. Beware of salespeople who voluntarily offer negative appraisals of the jewelry you are wearing. Not only are they acting unprofessionally when they claim that their merchandise is better quality and less expensive than everything you've purchased elsewhere, they're also degrading you as a buyer.

♦ What types of credentials do they have? Are they members of a professional trade organization such as the American Gem Society, Jewelers of America, the Canadian Jewellers' Association, the International Society of Appraisers, the American Society of Appraisers, or the National Association of Jewelry Appraisers? Have they earned titles or diplomas such as an FGA (Fellow of the Gemmological Association of Great Britain) or GG (Graduate Gemologist)?

♦ Are they only interested in making money, or do they also appreciate jewelry and enjoy servicing clients?

♦ Do you feel comfortable in the store? Is the atmosphere friendly and professional?

If you're satisfied with your answers to these questions, then you've found a jeweler that offers excellent service. Take advantage of it and establish a business relationship with him or her if you haven't already done so. There are lots of reliable jewelers. Sometimes, however, it's hard to find them when you need them.

15

How to Care for and Protect Your Diamond Ring

Cleaning Your Diamond Ring

Would you like your diamond ring to look better than many rings that are far more valuable? There's a simple formula--keep it clean. A clean imperfect diamond, for example, can look more attractive than a dirty flawless diamond. Yet, there may be thousands of dollars of difference between the two.

It's hard, however, to keep a diamond ring clean. Diamonds are natural grease attractors. In fact, diamonds are separated from other stones and dirt by passing mined material over a grease belt. Diamonds stick to the grease while the other stones and dirt are washed away. Consequently, diamonds can become coated with grease when they are immersed in dishwater or when they come in contact with any greasy substance including lotions and natural skin oils.

A safe and easy way to clean a diamond ring is to soak and wash it in warm sudsy water using a mild liquid detergent. Then it can be dried with a soft, lint-free cloth. Ethyl alcohol, ammonia solutions, and jewelry cleaning solutions may also be used for cleaning and soaking diamond jewelry. The alcohol has the advantage of evaporating quickly and not leaving water spots. Ammonia is not only good for cleaning diamonds; it's also good for brightening metals, particularly yellow gold. Alcohol and ammonia may damage other types of stones, so consult your jeweler before using them on anything but diamond jewelry. Do not use chlorine solutions to clean rings. The chlorine can pit and dissolve gold alloys. This pitting can also occur when rings are worn while swimming.

If the dirt on the diamond(s) cannot be washed off with a cloth after soaking, try using a tooth pick, a Water Pick, or unwaxed dental floss to remove caked-on dirt. Brushes should be used with caution because the bristles can scratch gold mountings.

Frequently, in order to get rid of encrusted dirt, rings must be cleaned professionally with steamers and ultrasonics (cleaning machines that can shake dirt loose with a vibrating detergent solution using high-frequency sound waves). Ultrasonic and steam cleaners should not be used for severely cracked diamonds or for gemstones such as opals, emeralds, pearls, coral, turquoise, malachite, tanzanite, moonstone, and lapis lazuli.

Sometimes it takes hours to effectively clean a diamond ring in an ultrasonic. There are times, however, when ultrasonics and steamers cannot get rid of dirt and metal residue. In these cases, the diamonds may have to be boiled in sulfuric acid. Lengthy and risky cleaning procedures can be avoided by cleaning jewelry on a regular basis. Once a week is not too often for a diamond ring that is worn daily.

Storing Your Diamond Ring

Protection from theft and damage should be prime considerations when storing a diamond ring. Jewelry boxes can protect a ring from damage if the ring is stored individually, but they are one of the first places burglars look when they break into a house. Therefore, it's best to reserve jewelry boxes for costume jewelry when they are displayed on tables or dressers.

Diamond rings should be wrapped separately in soft material or placed individually in pouches or the pockets of padded jewelry bags. If a diamond ring is placed next to or on top of other jewelry, the metal mountings or stones can get scratched. Use your imagination to find a secure place in your house to hide jewelry pouches, bags, and boxes. If a ring is seldom worn, it's best to keep it in a safe deposit box.

Preventing Your Diamonds from Being Switched

Stone switching is less common than many people think, but it does occasionally occur. Wondering if a stone has been or will be switched can be just as disturbing as actually having it switched. Use the following guidelines to help avoid unnecessary worry or false accusations and to prevent your diamond(s) from being switched when you have it repaired or appraised.

♦ Know your diamond(s). What color is it approximately? If there are several diamonds, are their colors the same? What types of clarity characteristics does it have--chips, scratches, naturals, clouds, feathers? Where are these clarity characteristics located on the diamond? What type of girdle does it have--bruted, faceted, or polished? Is the girdle thick or thin? Is the crown high or low? To determine these types of characteristics, no special instruments are needed except a loupe.

Diamond dealers and jewelers control stone switching by noting the weight, the measurements, and the price of diamonds. Writing or drawing the clarity and cutting characteristics of diamonds would be too time-consuming. Laypeople rarely have the scales and instruments needed to weigh and measure diamonds. They can, however, ask salespeople to write the weights on their sales receipts. The measurements of large diamonds can also be indicated. This information will then be available when needed.

♦ Keep the diamond(s) clean. This will help you recognize it. The color, clarity, and brilliance of a dirty diamond can change so much when it is cleaned that the owner may not believe the stone is the same.

♦ Have descriptive characteristics of your diamond(s) and ring written on both your copy and the store's copy of the take-in receipt. If you leave a diamond bracelet or necklace with someone, also have the length of the piece and the number of stones or links written on the receipt. It is normal for stores and appraisers to write *colorless stone* or *yellow metal* in place of *diamond* and *gold* if they don't have time to test the stone and the metal. It is normal too for them to refuse to indicate the color and clarity grade of a diamond on the take-in receipt, especially if it is mounted. Exact grades cannot be accurately assigned to mounted diamonds. Stores should, however, be willing to write down characteristics that are visible and measurable, if you ask them. Not only can written receipts serve as documentary evidence of switching, they can also help prevent it from occurring.

♦ If you have a diagram or photograph of your diamond(s) or ring, photocopy it and ask the store to acknowledge that it is a fair representation. The jewelry piece itself can also be photocopied.

♦ Beware of jewelers who do repairs for unbelievably low prices. Perhaps a lack of experience or honesty may be the reason for such low prices.

♦ Try to establish a relationship with a jeweler you feel is trustworthy. This is probably the best preventative of all.

16

Finding a Good Buy

SALE $1499
ONE-CARAT DIAMOND SOLITAIRE RINGS

Scott and Annemarie are looking through the newspaper and see this ad. It attracts their attention because they've been looking for a one-carat round diamond set in a simple solitaire ring. They have just finished reading *The Diamond Ring Buying Guide*.

Before reading the book, they would have thought that a one-carat ring for $1499 would be a great buy. Now they realize it could also be a poor buy because the ad says nothing about the quality of the diamond. All it tells them is that the $1499 solitaire rings are set with diamonds weighing approximately one carat.

Scott and Annemarie have already looked at rings in other stores but haven't seen anything with a one-carat diamond for as low as $1499, so out of curiosity, they decide to check out the sale. When they enter the store they are greeted by a friendly salesman named Adam. They notice a big difference in the diamonds Adam shows them from the ones they have seen in other stores. Some of these are gritty looking, others are milky white, some look chunky, all have eye-visible flaws, and none are colorless or near colorless.

Annemarie spots a yellowish diamond that is nicely proportioned and weighs 0.95 carats. She places it on her hand and is impressed with its brilliance and sparkle and the way its color harmonizes with her skin tone. Then she has Adam let her look at it through the microscope. There are no chips or big cracks and the black spots in it are not very prominent. In fact without the microscope, it's hard to see these spots.

Adam doesn't know the color or clarity grade of the diamond. He's just a student working his way through college. He's a lot more patient, pleasant, and straightforward, though, than some more knowledgeable salespeople they have met. Scott and Annemarie are happy with the diamond and with the 14K yellow gold mounting it comes with. The ring will go well with the diamond and the rest of her gold jewelry . They are glad they can find the size diamond they want at a price they can afford and that they are giving the sale to someone as nice and honest as Adam.

Tom and Erica are also attracted to the solitaire ring ad. They want to see what the $1499 rings look like, so they head to the store with the sale. Erica has learned a lot about diamonds from her mother, and both she and Tom have read *The Diamond Ring Buying Guide*. They don't like any of the diamonds that are on sale, so they ask to see some of better quality. To their surprise, the better diamonds cost more than those of comparable quality at some other stores they have been to.

Tom and Erica are discouraged and decide to go back to their family jeweler, Mr. Hall. Since their budget is limited and they want a colorless diamond, Mr. Hall suggests looking at a half-carat stone he recently bought at a public auction. It's an F color, SI clarity diamond, and it's exceptionally well cut. For its size and quality, it's the best price Tom and Erica have seen anywhere. Its only drawback is its size. After much shopping, they realize they'll have to wait before they can buy a diamond of both the size and quality they had originally planned on. As Mr. Hall points out, later they can trade it in on a larger diamond or have it mounted in a necklace or in a ring for Tom.

Erica is allergic to gold alloys, so platinum is a natural choice for the mounting. The platinum will compliment the color of her diamond and will give her a secure and long-wearing ring. Tom and Erica are glad they've found the color diamond they want at a price they can afford, and they're happy they're giving the sale to the jeweler that has given them and their families years of good service.

Erica and Annemarie have had very different experiences buying their diamond rings, but they've each received a good deal and a ring that they are happy with. However, it wasn't just by chance they got a good buy. Let's look at some of the guidelines that helped them and can help you.

♦ Know what types of diamond flaws and cutting defects to avoid. These are outlined in Chapters Six and Seven. Scott and Annemarie were able to look through a group of diamonds and find an acceptable one because they knew how to distinguish between good and poor quality. If you went to a meat market you'd never been to, you wouldn't expect the butcher to give you his leanest and most tender meat. Likewise, you shouldn't expect a jeweler who doesn't know you to show you his best diamond buys. Both have merchandise they need to get rid of. They will reserve their better merchandise for their regular customers or for people who recognize and ask for good quality. They will pass off their less desirable merchandise on customers interested in price rather than value.

♦ When judging prices, try to compare diamonds of the same shape, size, color, clarity, and cut quality. Compare mountings with the same metal type, weight, setting styles, and workmanship. All of these factors affect the cost of a diamond ring. Due to the complexity of jewelry pricing, it's easiest for a layperson to compare diamonds or rings that are alike.

♦ Compare per carat diamond prices, not stone prices (the total cost of a diamond). Chapter Four explains why.

♦ Look at several diamonds so you have a basis for comparison.

♦ Do not assume that all jewelers grade diamonds in the same way. Some jewelers are more strict than others, so grades can be misleading. That's why it's important for you to understand how to judge diamond quality and to look at diamonds under magnification before buying them. Even diamonds accompanied by grading reports or certificates should be viewed carefully by the buyer. Many of these written evaluations, even from reputable labs, do not give a good description of the quality of the cut or the degree of brilliance.

♦ Beware of sales or ads that seem too good to be true. The advertised merchandise might be of unacceptable quality or it might have been stolen or misrepresented. Jewelers are in business to make money not to lose it.

♦ Be willing to compromise. Both Annemarie and Erica had to make compromises in order to find a good buy and stay within their budget. Annemarie had to get a diamond with a lower clarity grade than she might have liked. Erica had to get a smaller diamond than she had planned on. Even people with unlimited budgets have to compromise sometimes on the size, shape, color, or quality they want due to lack of availability. A diamond doesn't have to be perfect for you to enjoy it.

♦ If possible, establish a relationship with a jeweler you can trust and who looks after your welfare. He can help you find buys that you wouldn't find on your own.

♦ Look at the diamond(s) on your hand as it would normally be viewed and answer the following questions. (A negative answer to any one of the questions suggests the diamond is a poor choice).

    a.   Is the diamond brilliant?
    b.   Does it sparkle?
    c.   Does it look good on your hand?
    d.   Does it look good compared to other diamonds of the same shape and size? Keep in mind that lighting can affect the appearance of diamonds so try to view them under different lights.

♦ Put the ring on your finger and answer the following questions. (Again, a negative answer suggests the ring is a poor choice).

    a.   Does it look good on your hand?
    b.   Does it feel good on your hand?
    c.   Is there a good chance that it will stay in style?
    d.   Does it fit your personality?
    e.   Is it practical for how you plan to wear it?

Scott & Annemarie and Tom & Erica are not gemologists or jewelers. Scott & Annemarie don't even know the exact color and clarity grades of the diamond they selected. Yet, both of these couples were able to find a diamond ring that's a good buy. So can you-- if you are willing to devote some time to determining your needs and to learning the fundamentals of diamond jewelry evaluation.

Perhaps some readers were expecting *The Diamond Ring Buying Guide* to tell them what is the best diamond, metal, and style, for their ring. There is no one diamond, metal, or style for all people. Choosing a diamond ring is a very personal matter. *The Diamond Ring Buying Guide* was written to help people make their own buying decisions, not to dictate what they should buy.

When you get a diamond ring, you're getting more than just a rock attached to a hunk of metal. You're getting a work of art that you can hold and wear. You're getting a symbol of beauty, purity, strength, and eternity. These symbolic associations are the result of the intrinsic characteristics of the ring materials.

Gold, platinum, and diamonds have a lot in common. In their pure state, they're all composed of a single atomic element; they're all chemically stable and will not tarnish or change with time; they're all rare and can be used as ornaments or as a medium of exchange; they're all important to the health and welfare of modern man because of their technical and industrial applications; they've all played an important role in the history of mankind.

Before the 1700's, only kings, queens, and other nobility were allowed to wear diamond rings. This is no longer an exclusive privilege. You can have the pleasure of wearing them and of giving them as pledges of love and commitment. Your diamond ring is very special, just like the person wearing it. So treasure it, take good care of it. If you do, it can bring you and your loved ones years of enjoyment.

Bibliography

Diamonds

Argenzio, Victor. *Diamonds Eternal*. New York: David McKay, 1974.

Bruton, Eric. *Diamonds*. Radnor, PA: Chilton, 1978.

Dickinson, Joan Younger. *The Book of Diamonds*. New York: Crown Publishers, 1965.

Friedman, Michael. *The Diamond Book*. Homewood, IL: Dow Jones-Irwin, 1980.

Gemological Institute of America. Diamond Course

Green, Timothy. *The World of Diamonds*. New York: William Morrow, 1981.

Kassoy Inc. *Everything You Always Wanted to Know about Diamonds*. New York: Kassoy Inc., 1977.

Pagel-Theisen, Verena. *Diamond Grading ABC*. New York: Rubin & Son, 1986.

Spero, Saul A. *Diamonds, Love, & Compatibility*. Hicksville, NY: Exposition Press, 1977.

Gold & Platinum

Branson, Oscar T. *What You Need to Know About Your Gold and Silver.* Tucson, AZ: Treasure Chest Publications, 1980.

Brod, I. Jack. *Consumer's Guide to Buying and Selling Gold, Silver, and Diamonds.* Garden City, NY: Doubleday, 1985.

Burkett, Russell. *Everything You Wanted to Know about Gold and Other Precious Metals.* Whittier, CA: Gem Guides Book Co., 1975.

Cavelti, Peter C. *New Profits in Gold, Silver & Strategic Metals.* New York: McGraw-Hill, 1985.

Merton, Henry A. *Your Gold & Silver.* New York: Macmillan, 1981.

Sutherland, C. H. V. *Gold Its Beauty, Power and Allure.* New York: McGraw-Hill, 1969.

Jewelry and Gems

Bovin, Murray. *Jewelry Making.* Forest Hills, NY: Bovin Publishing, 1967.

Gemological Institute of America. Appraisal Seminar handbook.

Gemological Institute of America. Gem Identification Course.

Gemological Institute of America. Jewelry Repair Workbook.

Gemological Institute of America. Jewelry Sales Course.

Jarvis, Charles A. *Jewelry Manufacture and Repair.* New York: Bonanza, 1979.

Liddicoat, Richard T. *Handbook of Gem Identification.* Santa Monica, CA: Gemological Institute of America, 1981.

Marcum, David. *Fine Gems and Jewelry.* Homewood, IL.: Dow Jones-Irwin, 1986.

Matlins, Antoinette L. & Bonanno, A. C. *Jewelry & Gems the Buying Guide.* South Woodstock, VT: Gemstone Press, 1987.

Miller, Anna M. *Gems and Jewelry Appraising.* New York: Van Nostrand Reinhold Company, 1988.

Morton, Philip. *Contemporary Jewelry.* New York: Holt, Rinehart, and Winston, 1976.

Preston, William S. *Guides for the Jewelry Industry.* New York: Jewelers Vigilance Committee, Inc., 1986.

Ramsey, John L. & Ramsey, Laura J. *The Collector/Investor Handbook of Gems.* San Diego, CA: Boa Vista Press, 1985.

Sarett, Morton R. *The Jewelry in Your Life.* Chicago: Nelson-Hall, 1979.

Schumann, Walter. *Gemstones of the World.* New York: Sterling 1977.

Sprintzen, Alice. *Jewelry Basic Techniques and Design.* Radnor, PA: Chilton, 1980

Untracht, Oppi. *Jewelry Concepts & Technology.* New York: Doubleday, 1982.

Von Neumann, Robert. *The Design and Creation of Jewelry.* Radnor, PA: Chilton, 1972.

Wykoff, Gerald L. *Beyond the Glitter.* Washington DC: Adamas, 1982.

Magazines

American Jewelry Manufacturer. Philadelphia, PA.

Gems and Gemology. Santa Monica, CA: Gemological Institute of America.

The Goldsmith. Atlanta, GA: Allen/Abernethy Division of A/S/M Communications Inc.

Jewelers Circular Keystone. Radnor, PA: Chilton Publishing Co.

Jewelers' Quarterly Magazine. Sonoma, CA.

Modern Jeweler. Lincolnshire, IL: Vance Publishing Inc.

National Jeweler. New York: Gralla Publications.

Science, Vol. 234. "Is Diamond the New Wonder Material?" Nov. 28, 1986.

Science News, Vol. 130. "Diamond Electronics: Sparkling Potential." Aug. 23, 1986.

Sky & Telescope. "Stardust on Earth." June 1987.

Index

Order Form

To: International Jewelry Publications
P.O. Box 13384
Los Angeles, CA 90013-0384   USA

Please send me:

___ copies of **THE DIAMOND RING BUYING GUIDE.**
Within California $14.02 each (includes sales tax)
All other destinations $12.95 US each

___ copies of **THE RUBY & SAPPHIRE BUYING GUIDE.**
Within California $21.60 each (includes sales tax)
All other destinations $19.95 US each

___ copies of **THE PEARL BUYING GUIDE**
Within California $20.51 each (includes sales tax)
All other destinations $18.95 US each

___ copies of **THE GOLD JEWELRY BUYING GUIDE** (available after Nov. 1993)
Within California $21.60 each (includes sales tax)
All other destinations $19.95 US each

Postage & Handling for Books

USA: first book $1.50, each additional copy $.75
Canada & foreign - surface mail: first book $2.50, ea. addl. $1.50
Canada & Mexico - airmail: first book $3.75, ea. addl. $2.50
All other foreign destinations - airmail: first book $9.00, ea. addl. $5.00

___ copies of **DIAMONDS: FASCINATING FACTS.**
Within California $4.28 each (includes sales tax)
All other destinations $3.95 US each

Postage for Diamonds: Fascinating Facts
USA: $0.55 per booklet
Canada & Mexico - airmail: $0.80 per booklet
All other foreign destinations - airmail: $1.25 per booklet

Total Amount Enclosed
(USA funds drawn on a USA bank)

Ship to:

Name_____

Address_____

City_____ State or Province_____

Postal or Zip Code_____ Country _____

Order Form

To: International Jewelry Publications
P.O. Box 13384
Los Angeles, CA 90013-0384 USA

Please send me:

____ copies of **THE DIAMOND RING BUYING GUIDE.**
Within California $14.02 each (includes sales tax)   _____
All other destinations $12.95 US each   _____

____ copies of **THE RUBY & SAPPHIRE BUYING GUIDE.**
Within California $21.60 each (includes sales tax)   _____
All other destinations $19.95 US each   _____

____ copies of **THE PEARL BUYING GUIDE**
Within California $20.51 each (includes sales tax)   _____
All other destinations $18.95 US each   _____

____ copies of **THE GOLD JEWELRY BUYING GUIDE** (available after Nov. 1993)
Within California $21.60 each (includes sales tax)   _____
All other destinations $19.95 US each   _____

Postage & Handling for Books

USA: first book $1.50, each additional copy $.75   _____
Canada & foreign - surface mail: first book $2.50, ea. addl. $1.50   _____
Canada & Mexico - airmail: first book $3.75, ea. addl. $2.50   _____
All other foreign destinations - airmail: first book $9.00, ea. addl. $5.00   _____

____ copies of **DIAMONDS: FASCINATING FACTS.**
Within California $4.28 each (includes sales tax)   _____
All other destinations $3.95 US each   _____

Postage for Diamonds: Fascinating Facts
USA: $0.55 per booklet   _____
Canada & Mexico - airmail: $0.80 per booklet   _____
All other foreign destinations - airmail: $1.25 per booklet _____

Total Amount Enclosed   _____
(USA funds drawn on a USA bank)

Ship to:

Name_____

Address_____

City_____ State or Province_____

Postal or Zip Code_____ Country _____

OTHER PUBLICATIONS BY RENEE NEWMAN

The Ruby & Sapphire Buying Guide:
How to Spot Value & Avoid Ripoffs

A guide to buying, evaluating, identifying, and caring for rubies and sapphires.

Discover:

- ♦ How to choose a good-quality stone
- ♦ How to tell a fake from a real ruby or sapphire
- ♦ How to compare prices and save money
- ♦ How to buy gems abroad

"Solid, informative and comprehensive . . . dissects each aspect of ruby and sapphire value in detail and quizzes the reader on key points at the end of each chapter. . . a wealth of grading information . . . *The Ruby & Sapphire Buying Guide* is a definite thumbs-up for both the unskilled and semiskilled buyer and seller. There is something here for everyone."
  C. R. Beesley, President, American Gemological Laboratories, New York. *Jewelers' Circular Keystone*

"Highly recommended . . . includes a great deal of gemmological as well as commercial information; text photographs are clear and cover many situations for appraisal which have rarely been put forward in gemmology texts before. . . . useful to the gemmology student as well as to the dealer or purchaser of jewelry."
  The Journal of Gemmology, a publication of the Gemmological Association of Great Britain

"Well-written--not so technical that you would need a dictionary to understand what is written and, most important, the information in it is all pertinent to anyone who wants to buy and sell colored gemstones. I have recommended this book to all my students and I enthusiastically recommend it to anyone interested in colored gemstones. Well done!"
  H. B. Leith, teacher-gemologist, master goldsmith

204 pages, 10 color and 86 black/white photos, 7" by 9", $19.95 US.

AVAILABLE AT bookstores, jewelry supply stores, the GIA, through the Jewelers' Book Club and *Lapidary Journal* or by mail: See reverse side for order form.

Diamonds: Fascinating Facts

An informative booklet with entertaining facts, poems, and statistics about diamonds.

A novel and appropriate greeting card to include with a diamond gift. It comes with a 6" x 9" white envelope. The inside front cover is designed to allow for a personal message.

Full-color, 16-page, self-cover booklet with six 5" x 7 1/2" photos, $3.95 US.

The Pearl Buying Guide:

This informative book explains and shows:

- ♦ How to judge pearl quality
- ♦ How imitation pearls differ from those that are real
- ♦ How cultured pearls differ from those that are natural
- ♦ How South Sea, freshwater, and Japanese saltwater pearls are valued
- ♦ How a simple pearl necklace can be a versatile piece of jewelry

An interesting and easy-to-understand guide to buying, evaluating, selecting, and caring for pearls and pearl jewelry. The opening chapters point out common mistakes made when evaluating or buying pearls and offer a compelling dialogue between the pearl family and pearl oysters, that clarifies curious facts about pearls. Other chapters focus on evaluating pearl types and shapes, luster, nacre thickness, color, flaws, size, weight, length and make. 1 Additional chapters cite differences in South Sea, black, and freshwater pearls a, as well as imitation, natural, and cultured pearls. The closing chapters highlight the proper way to care for pearls as well as creative ways to wear them. The many photographs are valuable in illustrating the characteristics of and differences among pearls. Overall, the guide is useful to all types. of readers, from the professional jeweler to the average patron...
Library Journal

186 pages, 7" X 9", 8 color and 90 black & white photos, $18.95 US.

The Gold Jewelry Buying Guide

A guide to evaluating, pricing, identifying, and caring for gold jewelry.

Learn:

- ♦ How to judge the quality of jewelry mountings and settings
- ♦ How to figure the value of the gold in your jewelry
- ♦ How to select gold chains and jewelry that lasts
- ♦ How to detect fake and underkarated gold
- ♦ How to compare prices of jewelry mountings and chains

To be released by November 1993.   Price: $19.95

AVAILABLE AT bookstores, jewelry supply stores, the GIA and *the Lapidary Journal &* Jeweler's Book Clubs, or by mail: See reverse side for order form.

Order Form

To: International Jewelry Publications
P.O. Box 13384
Los Angeles, CA 90013-0384   USA

Please send me:

___ copies of **THE DIAMOND RING BUYING GUIDE.**
Within California $14.02 each (includes sales tax)
All other destinations $12.95 US each   _____

___ copies of **THE RUBY & SAPPHIRE BUYING GUIDE.**
Within California $21.60 each (includes sales tax)
All other destinations $19.95 US each   _____

___ copies of **THE PEARL BUYING GUIDE**
Within California $20.51 each (includes sales tax)
All other destinations $18.95 US each   _____

___ copies of **THE GOLD JEWELRY BUYING GUIDE** (available after Nov. 1993)
Within California $21.60 each (includes sales tax)
All other destinations $19.95 US each   _____

Postage & Handling for Books

USA: first book $1.50, each additional copy $.75
Canada & foreign - surface mail: first book $2.50, ea. addl. $1.50   _____
Canada & Mexico - airmail: first book $3.75, ea. addl. $2.50   _____
All other foreign destinations - airmail: first book $9.00, ea. addl. $5.00 _____

___ copies of **DIAMONDS: FASCINATING FACTS.**
Within California $4.28 each (includes sales tax)
All other destinations $3.95 US each   _____

Postage for Diamonds: Fascinating Facts
USA: $0.55 per booklet   _____
Canada & Mexico - airmail: $0.80 per booklet   _____
All other foreign destinations - airmail: $1.25 per booklet   _____

Total Amount Enclosed   _____
(USA funds drawn on a USA bank)

Ship to:

Name_____

Address_____

City_____ State or Province_____

Postal or Zip Code_____ Country _____